TRAVELING IN THE SPIRIT

MADE SIMPLE

TRAVELING IN THE SPIRIT
MADE SIMPLE

Praying Medic

INKITY
PRESS™

Inkity Press™
137 East Elliot Road, #2292, Gilbert, AZ 85234

This book and other Inkity Press titles can be found at:
InkityPress.com and PrayingMedic.com

Available from Amazon.com, CreateSpace.com, and other retail outlets.

For more information visit our website at **www.inkitypress.com**
or email us at **admin@inkitypress.com** or **admin@prayingmedic.com**

ISBN-13: 978-0998091204 (Inkity Press)
ISBN-10: 0998091200

Printed in the U.S.A.

THIS BOOK IS DEDICATED TO my friend Todd Adams who has, from the beginning, encouraged me to pursue God's heart about spiritual travel. There were many times when it seemed this book would never be completed. But Todd always believed in me, prayed for me and helped me cut a path through the jungle until at last, the journey was completed.

....

ACKNOWLEDGMENTS

I HAVE MANY FRIENDS WHO have graciously shared their experiences with traveling in the spirit during my public discussions both online and at meetings. What I've learned from those conversations has been encouraging and enlightening. This book would not have been possible without the contributions of hundreds of people who braved public criticism to share their stories. I'm grateful to everyone who participated in those discussions.

For providing their personal testimonies for this book, I'd like to thank Ben Swett, Brook Magar, Bryan Parks, Daniel Bryant Cook, Del Hungerford, Fern Pope, Gale Gibson, Katie Regan, Kellie Gordley Fitzgerald, Lisa Perna, Margie Moorman, Michelle Myers, Rebecca Clayton, Terry Mingus, Tom and Pat Calkins, and Mitzi Hanna.

I'd like to acknowledge the help of my friend Michael Van Vlymen, author of *Supernatural Transportation*. Although we worked on our respective books at the same time, we've never seen each other as competitors, but rather as friends. Our conversations have been instrumental in helping me complete this book.

I'm grateful to all my friends who have encouraged and prayed for me. I'd especially like to thank Anna Wingate, Anthony Murray, David McLain, Jesse Birkey, Jeremy Mangerchine, Michael King, Paul & Ginny Wilcox and Todd Adams.

A handful of leaders have pioneered the study of spiritual travel. The information they've provided has shed light on a path that's been shrouded in darkness for too long. I'd like to thank Bruce Allen, Grant Mahoney, Ian Clayton, Justin Abraham, Mike Parsons and Robert Henderson.

I'd like to thank my wife for her editorial help and for her design of the book cover and interior. She's also been my biggest cheerleader and best friend.

There is some difficulty in making abstract spiritual concepts relatable to those who are unfamiliar with them. It was particularly difficult to write about spiritual travel in a way that would allow the average person to understand it. I'm grateful to my friend and editor Lydia Blain for asking the difficult questions that needed to be asked and for insisting that I further explain concepts that were unclear. If you need help editing a writing project (large or small) you might contact Lydia through her website: http://lydiaedits.com/

"THE FINEST EMOTION OF WHICH WE ARE CAPABLE is the mystic emotion. Herein lies the germ of all art AND ALL TRUE SCIENCE. ANYONE TO WHOM THIS feeling is alien, who is no longer capable of wonderment AND LIVES IN A STATE OF FEAR IS A DEAD MAN. To know that what is impenetrable for us really exists and MANIFESTS ITSELF AS THE HIGHEST WISDOM AND the most radiant beauty, whose gross forms alone are INTELLIGIBLE TO OUR POOR FACULTIES—THIS knowledge, this feeling. . . that is the core of the true religious SENTIMENT. IN THIS SENSE, AND IN THIS SENSE alone, I rank myself among profoundly religious men."

~ ALBERT EINSTEIN

FOR SEVERAL YEARS, GOD HAS been speaking to me about traveling in the spirit. Information on this subject written from a Christian perspective is hard to find, so it seemed good to share what I've learned so far about the practice of spiritual travel. My desire with all the books in *The Kingdom of God Made Simple* series is to *simplify* complex spiritual ideas. This book will give you a basic understanding of the spiritual realms and provide practical instruction on how to navigate them safely.

We all receive instruction from God in our own unique ways. I rely heavily on my dreams. God speaks to me frequently about His kingdom and my place in it through them. In this book, I'll share a number of dreams I've had which illustrate different aspects of traveling in the spirit and how God wants me to teach on this subject. Some may not be accustomed to receiving revelation and instruction through dreams. All I ask is that you be patient with me as I unravel them. I'll let you decide if they are merely dreams or something more.

This book is not intended for everyone. Even if you find the testimonies and lessons in this book to be fascinating, there is a world of difference between having a fascination about something and making the commitment to make it a part of your daily life. The things you are about to read will require you to make a few choices—the consequences of which may be life-changing. Once I embraced the things I've written about in this book, I knew my life would never be the same.

A few years ago I had a dream that illustrated something about the audience this book is likely to impact. In the dream, I walked through a building that was long and narrow. It was filled with Christians who were eating at a banquet table. The building itself was white in color and resembled the models I've seen of the tabernacle of Moses. There were many types of food available at this banquet, but each person had chosen to eat only one type of food. I made note of this, but continued straight through the building and entered a second building and then took an elevator to the second floor. When I exited the elevator, I went into a gymnasium where I saw people playing volleyball. I joined them and when it was my turn to serve the ball, I hit it over the net. When I did, no one on the other side could hit the ball back. Some of my serves dropped just over the net, while others curved as they approached people, so they could not be returned. Near the end of this scene, I served a loaf of bread wrapped in aluminum foil to a woman. It curved away from her as she tried to hit it. She picked it up then walked over and asked how I made it do that. At this point, I left the gymnasium and went back through the long white building and then found myself at an ocean beach. I scanned the shore, but only found a few teenagers at the beach. I walked over to them and struck up a conversation. As I talked, I could see that where the water met the land, the water was at least 20 feet deep. I told the teenagers the water was very deep where it met the land and I suggested they jump in. They didn't believe me and thought I was crazy, so I decided to show them it was safe. I saw a lifeguard stand nearby. I climbed to the top of the stand then jumped off into the water, right where it met the sand. I plunged down into deep water. When I surfaced, I was laughing. I told them it was perfectly safe to jump in and they joined me.

This dream illustrates a number of things. First, it reveals three types of experiences people have in "the church." The first is the broader type of experience most believers have, when they attend a weekly church service to be "fed" by a pastor. There isn't much that's exciting about this type of spiritual life. There is no condemnation for those who are satisfied to live this way, though the dream does suggest there is more available to these believers than they're aware of, or choose to partake in.

The second scene, where the people were playing volleyball, may illustrate a smaller group of people who "exercise" the gifts of the spirit. There is no criticism or condemnation toward this group either, but there does seem to be more available to them as well. The fact that they could not receive the "bread" I served seems to suggest they may not be the main audience I'm supposed to reach.

The third scene illustrated a small group of people who may have at some point participated in these activities, but now live on the fringes of Christianity. They've found the typical Christian experience to be too shallow and boring. They were looking for something deeper—something more meaningful—and so was I. When I arrived at the place where the sea met the land, I saw the unlimited possibilities of the spiritual realm and realized this was what I had been looking for. The teenagers were also hungry for an experience that was deeper, but they sensed danger. I knew there was no *real* danger—only a perceived one. I encouraged them to take a chance. By my own example, I proved that their fears were unfounded and led them into a deeper experience in the kingdom.

From this dream, I learned that the experiences and revelation God gives me are intended to help train and equip a rather small group of people. And while my message may be heard by folks outside of this small group, the things I write are not actually intended for them. My guess is that they will not bear fruit from what they read. I'd like to explain why this is so.

The first book in this series is on divine healing. After it was published, I heard back from readers who—after sharing what they had learned with their pastors—were sternly warned not to talk about such foolishness at their church. Some dared to go into their communities and heal the sick. When they came back and told their leaders what had happened, they were rejected. Some were asked not to come back to their church.

Subjects like healing and seeing in the spirit are not taught in seminaries and Bible colleges. This means many church leaders have no training in these areas and no theological grid for understanding them. Problems arise when sheep begin learning about things their shepherds are not familiar with. A humble leader might be expected to further his understanding of these things in order to help the sheep grow, but humility and leadership don't always go together. While some leaders are open to these things because they're also hungry for all that God has for us, other leaders feel pressed to silence the sheep who threaten to overturn their apple cart. If things as simple as divine healing and seeing visions are perceived by church leaders as a threat, what do you imagine they will do when the sheep begin talking about traveling in the spirit?

If you regularly attend a church, you might give some thought to what your leaders would say if you were to tell them about your interest in spiritual travel. If they're like many leaders, their reaction is not going to be favorable. If you find that you can talk to them about it, you are among the fortunate few. Consider the possibility that you may be the one leading the discussion, and if there's sufficient interest, you may find yourself in the role of teacher. But if your leaders are not open to such discussions, you may want to get in touch with some who are. Having a support group when you're operating in the supernatural is essential. You'll want to connect with people who are interested, and ideally—experienced. It may take a while to find them, so if this is something you plan to make a part of your daily life, you may want to begin looking now.

All of this may seem too daunting a task. It's both difficult and dangerous to live a deeply spiritual life apart from others who are like-minded. If you're not willing to find people who can help you grow, you're likely to either give up somewhere along the way or have something go terribly wrong. (I'll provide resources throughout the book where you can find others who are interested in this subject.)

No doubt, some will be concerned that this book is an attempt to distract believers away from their primary focus of Jesus Christ, His resurrection, and His life fulfilled in them. Let me say this about the purpose of this book: My *only* purpose for writing this book is that I might assist you in developing a deeper and more meaningful relationship with your savior. Everything in this book is written for the express purpose of encouraging you to grow into a stronger, more vibrant relationship with Jesus. It is my belief that the very purpose of spiritual travel is to deepen our relationship with our Creator. My own travels in the spiritual realm have indeed drawn me closer to Him.

Despite this, I know there are many who will have concerns that this book will cause believers to focus on non-essential (or even dangerous) practices. There is a legitimate concern that books like this one will cause spiritual travel to become an unhealthy obsession that will lead some into error.

Virtually any good thing can become an obsession and an unhealthy preoccupation if prioritized wrongly. In most cases, it is not a question of whether the practice itself is dangerous, but whether the individual has the right motives in their heart, a wise support group from which to take direction, and a sound relationship with God—where they are kept safe through His correction. When a believer develops an unhealthy preoccupation, it is usually done in a setting where they are either isolated or spiritually immature—or both. The voices of correction that would normally keep them out of trouble are either not heard or not heeded. Books on this subject must be written for the benefit of those who are interested in growing in spiritual maturity, despite the fact that some will use the information unwisely.

Traveling in the spirit is not something that interested me until God brought it up in our conversations and in my dreams. Being a former atheist, I'm not overly curious about the supernatural. Learning about traveling in the spirit was not my idea. It was God's idea. In fact, most of the Christians I know who are learning about it had no interest in the subject until God began speaking to them about it or giving them experiences.

One of the surprising things I learned while hosting public discussions on spiritual travel is how many people had already been having these experiences, but did not understand their purpose and many times, did not know they were from God. As the body of Christ focuses more of its attention on the manifestation of God's kingdom, believers appear to be having more experiences of spiritual travel. At some point, Christian authors need to at least attempt to explain these phenomena and provide some biblical instruction for those who have had the experiences already or who soon will be having them. I believe spiritual travel is of greater interest to God than it is to us and I believe it's our collective lack of understanding that prevents us from more effectively operating in these things.

When the Holy Spirit suggested I write this book, my initial reaction was concern. I felt I was unqualified for the task. He reminded me that I didn't need to have all the answers in order to write a competent book on this subject. What I needed was to understand the basic principles, to know what the Bible teaches on it, and to share some personal experiences along with the testimonies of others. And that is exactly what this book is. I'll outline the biblical position on spiritual travel, I'll share my own experiences and the experiences of others, and I'll do my best to explain in layman's terms some of the basic principles of spiritual travel.

The intent of this book is to give you a place to begin your travels with God, or, if you're already having them, to gain a better understanding of those experiences. As you have these experiences, it's imperative that you ask Him to teach you the reasons why He wants you to travel, and how to do it safely. As far as safety is concerned, I will propose some guidelines, but ultimately each person should develop their own protocol with the Holy Spirit's guidance.

There will be many words of caution in this book and here is one I cannot overemphasize:

If you are not certain that you're hearing the Holy Spirit clearly and consistently, you may be wise to wait until you've had time to better develop your ability to hear from Him. (When I say "hear from Him" I'm using this in the broadest way possible, as many people receive communication from God in ways other than by hearing.)

Much of what we perceive to be spiritual travel comes to us in the form of visions or impressions from other spiritual senses. It is possible to travel in the spirit without having well-developed spiritual senses, but if you're able to see, feel, hear, and sense things in the spirit, traveling becomes more meaningful. If you're not able to sense things in the spirit very well, you're going to be at a disadvantage.

I would consider the subject of this book to be an advanced level of instruction. It contains material that may not be easily understood or practiced by new believers. For that reason, I would advise readers to exercise caution before engaging in spiritual travel. Some may do it safely, while others will encounter problems due to their spiritual immaturity. I will provide some basic instruction and exercises designed to help develop your spiritual senses, but if you need more help, I have books available on hearing God's voice and seeing in the spirit.

Most of the articles on the Internet equate Christian spiritual travel with astral projection and don't offer an intelligent explanation for either one. For years, if a believer wanted to understand spiritual travel they were forced to learn about it through websites devoted to teaching astral projection or they'd have to dig through ancient texts written by Christian mystics who lived centuries ago. The former was the easier choice, though the latter was a much safer option.

I've discovered that most Christian authors today who write on astral projection and Christian spiritual travel make no attempt to distinguish the differences between them. They tend to lump them into the same category and declare them off limits. There is a pervasive lack of understanding about this subject among leaders in the body of Christ—even among my own peers in the Charismatic church, who might be expected to know more about it.

The church seems to have developed a case of collective amnesia about how and why spirit travel is done. I believe God wants to restore this mode of transportation that was once commonly used by prophets, the disciples, and Jesus. Because it's been so long since traveling in the spirit was commonplace, it's going to take time before we regain our understanding of it. The reality is—traveling in the spirit has always been available for believers to use; we've just been ignorant for too long about how to do it.

Although this subject is not well-understood by many Christians, there are some who have a good understanding of its principles and they've had some valuable experiences that are worth learning from. They've had instruction from God about the purpose for it, how it is done, and what the rules are for doing it. Yes, there are some rules that you'll need to learn and follow if you want to do this safely. I would be negligent to let you think there is no risk involved in spiritual travel. But if you learn the basic principles and get to know the leading of the Holy Spirit, you can learn to travel with minimal risk to yourself.

If you're ready to learn, we'll begin the first lesson, where we'll debunk some of the most common myths and misconceptions about traveling in the spirit.

~ Praying Medic

PART ONE
Can We Travel in the Spirit?

CHAPTER ONE

Misconceptions and Myths

IN THIS SECTION OF THE book, Part One, I'll provide background information that will lay a foundation for the discussions that will come in later chapters. In order for some to even entertain the idea that God might approve of traveling in the spirit, we must address the concerns and objections people have. We'll examine those objections, as well as the biblical narrative on spiritual travel, and the purposes God might have for it.

When I use the term "traveling in the spirit" in this book, I'm using it in the broadest sense. There are many ways in which one may "travel in the spirit," including (but not limited to) travel during dreams, translation by faith, when in a trance, and when the physical body is moved by God to another location. I consider all of these to be forms of traveling in the spirit. These methods will be addressed separately in their own chapters.

One of the main goals of this book is to help clear up some of the confusion and misinformation that exists about traveling in the spirit. Over the years, well-meaning leaders intending to safeguard the flock have created a pervasive belief system that opposes any kind of spiritual travel. In this chapter, I'll address some of the most common objections people have raised concerning traveling in the spirit.

"Spiritual travel is not taught in the Bible."

Many have argued that since the Bible doesn't explicitly teach that we should seek experiences that involve spiritual travel, it must be wrong or evil to do so. My answer to this objection is simple: Jesus taught in the Sermon on the Mount that we should seek first the kingdom of God (Mt 6:33.) This is about as explicit an instruction as you will ever hear from the Lord. He specifically (and imperatively) urged His disciples to seek and prioritize most highly, the things that pertain to the kingdom of God. The kingdom of God is first and foremost the invisible spiritual kingdom of angels and other heavenly beings we encounter while engaging the spiritual realm. If you ask 100 believers on any given day how they experienced the kingdom of God, you're likely to find many who say they haven't experienced it, or at least not in a way they can explain. The easiest and most effective way to seek and experience God's spiritual kingdom is to engage it directly through our spirit.

The apostle Paul wrote to the church in Corinth, encouraging them to seek the things of the invisible realm:

> ... *we do not look at the things which are seen, but at the things which are not seen. For the things which are seen are temporary, but the things which are not seen are eternal.*
> 2 COR 4:18

This instruction from Paul is counterintuitive, as our tendency is to focus on that which we can see. Yet Paul urges us to focus on the eternal unseen realm of the spirit. He wrote a similar exhortation to the church in Colossae, teaching them that the invisible things of the heavenly realm are the things they ought to seek:

Set your mind on things above, not on things on the earth.
COL 3:2

It may be argued that there are no explicit instructions in the Bible telling us to become proficient in spiritual travel. However, the prophets and apostles demonstrated spiritual travel often, and much of what they learned about God and His kingdom came from their travels in the spiritual world. In the scriptures, there is a constant emphasis on viewing life and the cosmos from the heavenly realm—something that is difficult to do if one has never been there.

I spoke with a man, who objected to spiritual travel because, as he put it: "Traveling in the spirit was not a regular part of the life of any of the disciples of Jesus." It's difficult to say with certainty how often first century believers engaged the spiritual realm, but we do know that the Apostle John was acquainted with spiritual travel. Most of the book of Revelation was written from the experiences he had while traveling in the spiritual realm of heaven.

"Traveling in the spirit is usually done for the wrong reasons."

Another objection to spiritual travel is that those who have these experiences are doing them for the wrong reasons and therefore, they are demonic in origin. While it is true that some people have wrong motives, there are many who have perfectly valid motives for spiritual travel. The impure motives of some do not negate the pure motives of others. The motive a person has in their heart for a certain experience does not by itself make the experience evil. There have been times when I healed the sick, not because I wanted to advance God's kingdom, or because I was filled with compassion, but because I needed a story to write for my blog. Although my own motives may have been less than honorable, God (not Satan) was the one who healed the people I prayed for. In a similar way, the fact that a person may have less than honorable motives for spiritual travel, does not mean their experience is demonic. Having pure motives makes you less susceptible to the influence of evil spirits, but even if your motives are not pristine, you can still have real (and many times positive) encounters with the Lord.

If one were to seek such an experience to increase their faith or to deepen their knowledge of God and His supernatural kingdom, how is this activity in any way evil?

"Spiritual travel is the wrong way to connect with God."

Encountering the kingdom of God and the spiritual world through spiritual travel may well be the most direct path to a strong and lasting relationship with Jesus. Many have come to their initial knowledge of God through such experiences. The Apostle Peter's understanding that the gospel was for the Gentiles came when he was in a trance. Most of the book of Revelation was written from John's experiences in the spiritual realm. Objecting to these experiences as being the wrong method is like a fire Captain reprimanding a firefighter for putting out a dumpster fire with a garden hose instead of the hose attached to the fire engine. For some, spiritual travel will always be the wrong method, even if it leads to the right answer—a deeper relationship with God. Some will always refuse to accept spiritual travel as a legitimate experience, regardless of the fruit that it bears. As with all that we do, it is the fruit produced by an experience that must be used to evaluate the origin of the experience itself, and not our preconceived ideas about methods and motives. Given the lack of authentic spirituality in the church today, we may be wise not to be too picky about *how* people arrive at their faith in God. Rather, we ought to focus on the goal of growing in faith, even if the methods we use seem a bit unconventional.

I will warn readers that there are methods of spiritual travel that can be dangerous. Methods *do* matter. Those methods will be covered extensively in later chapters. The point here is that spiritual travel itself should not be viewed exclusively as a tool of the enemy simply because we don't trust someone's motives or methods.

"Spirit travel is an occult experience."

It's common to take experiences that are not considered normal by mainstream Christian standards and categorize them as pagan or occult practices. The use of Tarot cards, Ouija boards, séances, casting spells, and spiritual travel are all considered to be occult experiences by a large section of the church. Critics of spiritual travel most commonly cite the following passage from the book of Deuteronomy as a prohibition:

> *Let no one be found among you who sacrifices his son or daughter in the fire, who practices divination or sorcery, interprets omens, engages in witchcraft, or casts spells, or who is a medium or spiritist or who consults the dead.*
> DEUT 18:10-11 NIV

Of all the experiences described in this book, none fit into any of the categories mentioned in this passage, with the possible exception of "consulting with the dead" which will be covered in a separate chapter. Spiritual travel as described in this book does not include the use of divination, the use of mediums, spiritism, casting spells, the interpretation of omens, or the practice of human sacrifice. This leaves the categories of sorcery, witchcraft, and the occult.

The concepts of the occult, sorcery, and witchcraft are used today to describe almost any practice one believes to be "non-Christian." Since these terms can include virtually any religious or spiritual activity that mainstream Christianity does not approve of, they've become almost meaningless. Because the definition of witchcraft was so vague centuries ago, thousands of true Christians were convicted of being witches and burned at the stake or drowned. The medieval church courts finally determined that there was no way to defend oneself against the charge of witchcraft and the same is true today. One can travel to the throne room of heaven to meet with the Lord every night and still be accused of sorcery or witchcraft. What constitutes sorcery or witchcraft today can be anything from celebrating Halloween or Christmas to playing rock and roll music.

"The spiritual travel in the Bible was always controlled by God."

When I began hosting public discussions about spirit travel, the vast majority of my Christian friends said it was their belief that the difference between spiritual travel as practiced by Christians, and that which was practiced by New Agers was that God was always the initiator of the Christian's experience, while New Agers initiated their own experiences. Some went one step further, saying that God not only had to initiate the experience, but that He always had to be in control of it.

This response reveals a few things about the Christian culture and how we view the supernatural. As a group, we greatly distrust our own ability to discern what is of God and what is not. The tendency to need some kind of tool or litmus test by which to judge supernatural experiences reveals the fact that we don't trust ourselves to make good decisions. We prefer to have a fool-proof mechanism in place that makes the decision for us. This is not surprising since much of mainstream Christian teaching places a heavy emphasis on the dangers of being deceived. Now it's not without cause that we fear deception. Jesus repeatedly warned His disciples not to be deceived. But the context of the Lord's warnings were generally not in reference to supernatural experiences. More often, He warned them about the dangers of following religious teachers who wanted to bring them under the law. The believer is supposed to live their life by faith. Fear is the opposite of faith. Many of us unknowingly live in constant fear of making wrong decisions.

I was surprised when I studied the spiritual travels of Elijah and Elisha. Contrary to what most Christians would like to believe, their experiences were as a rule, initiated by them and not God. We'll discuss their specific cases in the next chapter, but for now I would simply like to say that with few exceptions, the experiences of spiritual travel recorded in the Bible were initiated and controlled by man and not God.

"I don't see how traveling in the spirit glorifies God."

Part of the Westminster confession states: "The chief end of man is to glorify God..." This belief, though it may be true, may cause us to evaluate every theological point on the basis of whether or not it brings glory to God. Or rather, on whether we *believe* it does. The trouble isn't the idea that the creation should glorify God, but the suggestion that we can know with certainty which things bring glory to Him, and which do not. If you had never read the Psalms, would you conclude that trees clapping their hands, birds singing, and stars shining would bring glory to God? You probably wouldn't, but we know from the scriptures that God can be glorified by both the mundane and the spectacular.

Years ago, when I was learning to operate in the miraculous, I developed a habit of sticking coins to walls by the power of God. Many of my Christian friends objected to this practice. They didn't understand why God would "need" to stick a coin to the wall. Some objected because they could not see how it brought Him glory. But some of my non-Christian friends took it as a sign of His power. An EMT that I worked with asked how I did it. I explained that it's partly done by inviting God's presence into the room and partly by activating my faith and trusting He's going to make the coin stick to the wall. This simple object lesson helped him connect with God in a more meaningful way. Did God *need* to stick coins to the wall? Probably not. But the practice helped me develop faith for greater miracles and it helped my coworker see the power of God at work.

How was God glorified by Peter attempting to walk on water, but nearly drowning? Why did Jesus need to translocate into a room instead of using the door? Must we understand every theological detail of a supernatural experience before accepting it? If God's ways are not our ways, it may be safe to assume we will not always understand His purposes or what it is that brings Him glory.

Many of us are by nature suspicious of the supernatural. Some believe Satan is more supernatural than God. God is by nature supernatural in everything He does. Jesus is the best representation we have of the Father and He was known for performing miracles, healing the sick, casting out demons, and raising the dead. Being supernatural came naturally to Him and it brought glory to the Father. We are most like Him when we love others unconditionally and when we live supernaturally. I don't believe we can know this side of eternity which things glorify God and which do not. He is the only one who knows such things.

CHAPTER TWO

The Biblical Basis for Traveling in the Spirit

YOU MAY NOT THINK TRAVELING in the spirit is supported by the scriptures. It hasn't been the focus of Bible commentaries, nor has it been the subject of Sunday sermons. It certainly isn't taught in most seminaries. And although it's been ignored by teachers and believers for centuries, there is a surprising amount of scripture that either describes or teaches the principles of spiritual travel. In this chapter, we'll look at what can be learned about it from the Bible. I'll present a number of passages from the scriptures and provide commentary on how they relate to traveling in the spirit.

1 Kings Chapter 18

The eighteenth chapter of the book of first Kings contains a fascinating interaction between the prophet Elijah and Obadiah. The word of the Lord had come to Elijah, saying that the drought which the prophet had prophesied was coming to an end. Obadiah had been serving King Ahab, who sent him to find pasture for their animals. Elijah met Obadiah on the road and sent him to tell Ahab where he was. Apparently, Obadiah knew that Elijah had been physically moved by God as he confronted the prophet about his fear that if he told the king where Elijah was—he would disappear and go somewhere else:

> *And now you say, 'Go, tell your master, "Elijah is here"'! And it shall come to pass, as soon as I am gone from you, that the Spirit of the LORD will carry you to a place I do not know; so when I go and tell Ahab, and he cannot find you, he will kill me.*
> 1 KGS 18:11-12

This passage clearly indicates that Elijah had been traveling supernaturally to different locations in his physical body under the direction of God.

2 Kings Chapter 5

The fifth chapter of second Kings contains an account that can only be interpreted as a case of the prophet Elisha traveling in the spirit. Naaman, the Syrian General, had come down with leprosy. Elisha volunteered to heal him, but instead of meeting with the General in person, he sent his servant Gehazi to tell Naaman to wash himself in the Jordan. The General was outraged at this, but he grudgingly obeyed and was healed. After he was healed, Naaman offered gifts to Elisha, which the prophet refused. Naaman then left, but the prophet's servant, Gehazi, soon followed him and asked for silver and garments. The General gladly gave them to Gehazi, who stored them away before returning to the house of Elisha. When he arrived there, Elisha asked where he had gone. Gehazi lied, saying he went nowhere. Elisha then said:

> *"Did not my heart go with you when the man turned back from his chariot to meet you?"*
> 2 KGS 5:26

The word in this verse that is translated "heart" can also be translated "inner man" or "spirit." Elisha informed Gehazi that he had secretly traveled with him (in the spirit) to witness the transaction between him and Naaman.

Many would say that if spiritual travel were sanctioned by God, it should only be done under His sovereign control. They believe we cannot safely do it by exercising our own free will. This passage clearly illustrates a case where a man (a prophet of God no less) exercised his free will to travel in the spirit to observe one of his servants. It does not appear to be a case where God initiated the travel or controlled it. Elisha simply used his ability to travel in the spirit to eavesdrop on his servant's activities. As uncomfortable as it can be to know that we can travel in the spirit at will, even if at times it seems unwise or selfish, that is the freedom God has given us. (We will discuss this in more detail in another chapter.)

2 Kings Chapter 6

The sixth chapter of second Kings describes another account of spiritual travel involving the prophet Elisha. The prophet had been receiving information on the position of the Syrian King's troop placement when the two nations were at war. The knowledge that Israel had was so accurate, the Syrian King suspected that someone in his own camp was giving information to them. He asked his servants who the traitor was. One of the servants said there was no traitor, explaining:

"... the prophet who is in Israel, tells the king of Israel the words that you speak in your bedroom."
2 KGS 6:12

The servant said it was Elisha who had somehow learned the secrets the king only spoke about in private. It's impossible to say with certainty *how* Elisha received this inside information, but since we already know he was adept at using spirit travel to spy on his own servants, the most likely explanation is that the prophet traveled in the spirit to the king's bedroom to listen in on his private conversations.

The same principle is being used today by many governments around the world. The U.S. Department of Defense has protocols in place that use a form of spiritual travel to spy on its enemies. The practice, known as "remote viewing," has been in use for many years by a number of governments around the world. This ability enables the individual to see and hear things that are taking place a great distance from where their body is physically located.

Ezekiel Chapter 3

One of the most well-known cases of spiritual travel is recorded in the third chapter of Ezekiel. God had commissioned the prophet to speak to the people of Israel, who were in captivity. He then picked up Ezekiel and transported his physical body to the location where the people were being held captive, so that he might deliver a message:

> *So the Spirit lifted me up and took me away. I went in bitterness and turmoil, but the Lord's hold on me was strong. Then I came to the colony of Judean exiles in Tel-abib, beside the Kebar River. I was overwhelmed and sat among them for seven days.*
> EZEK 3:14-15 NLT

This appears to be a sovereign act of God, where Ezekiel was transported in his physical body for the purpose of delivering a message to the captives. A similar experience is recorded in Ezekiel 8:1-6 and another is recorded in Ezekiel chapter 40.

John Chapter 6

The sixth chapter of John contains a fascinating description of an event that seems to be a case where all twelve disciples of Jesus were supernaturally transported a distance of at least three miles:

> *Now when evening came, His disciples went down to the sea, got into the boat, and went over the sea toward Capernaum. And it was already dark, and Jesus had not come to them. Then the sea arose because a great wind was blowing. So when they had rowed about three or four miles, they saw Jesus walking on the sea and drawing near the boat; and they were afraid. But He said to them,*

"It is I; do not be afraid." Then they willingly received Him into the boat, and immediately the boat was at the land where they were going.
JN 6:16-21

After sending the disciples out onto the Sea, Jesus appeared to them in the middle of the night, walking on the waves. The narrative states that the group had rowed about three or four miles. (The Sea of Galilee is approximately nine miles at its widest from east to west.) This places them roughly in the middle of the Sea when the Lord appeared to them. The interesting thing to note is the last sentence, which indicates that after He entered the boat, it was immediately at shore. One minute they were close to the middle of the sea and the next they were at their destination.

John Chapter 20

In the following passage, Jesus is reported to have appeared to the disciples after He was resurrected. John specifically notes in his account that the doors to the room were shut—suggesting that the Lord must have either traveled through a wall or translocated into the room to be with them.

"And after eight days His disciples were again inside, and Thomas with them. Jesus came, the doors being shut, and stood in the midst, and said, "Peace to you!" Then He said to Thomas, "Reach your finger here, and look at My hands; and reach your hand here, and put it into My side. Do not be unbelieving, but believing."
JN 20:26-27

Luke Chapter 4

In Luke chapter four, there is an account of a mob that attempted to throw Jesus over a cliff because they were incensed by what He taught:

When they heard this, the people in the synagogue were furious. Jumping up, they mobbed him and forced him to the edge of the hill

on which the town was built. They intended to push him over the
cliff, but he passed right through the crowd and went on his way.
LUKE 4:28-30 NLT

Not only did Jesus resist the actions of this mob of angry Jews, He pulled
off a little spiritual sleight-of-hand to make His escape. Although He
was vastly outnumbered, He was somehow able to move through the
crowd in such a way that they could not grab hold of Him. It does not
seem as though the Lord became completely invisible. Those present
could plainly see Him as He moved through the crowd, though no one
could apprehend Him. You must admit, if you were ever in danger for
your life it would be helpful if you could move through a crowd the
way Jesus did.

Acts Chapter 8

One of the most well-known passages describing the physical transport of a believer is found in the book of Acts. Phillip had gone to
assist an Ethiopian eunuch who was reading a scroll of Isaiah. Phillip
explained the passage the eunuch was reading and the eunuch asked if
he might be baptized. Immediately after Phillip baptized him, he was
carried physically to another location to continue preaching:

> *So he commanded the chariot to stand still. And both Philip and*
> *the eunuch went down into the water, and he baptized him. Now*
> *when they came up out of the water, the Spirit of the Lord caught*
> *Philip away, so that the eunuch saw him no more; and he went*
> *on his way rejoicing. But Philip was found at Azotus. And passing*
> *through, he preached in all the cities till he came to Caesarea.*
> ACTS 8:38-40

Although it might seem bizarre at first, many believers today have been
physically moved to other parts of their city or to other countries to do
things God wanted them to do. All the testimonies of this kind that I've
heard would be considered sovereign acts of God. I have yet to meet
anyone who has been able to physically transport their body at will.
I don't think this means there is no chance for us to learn how to
do it. If it's possible to travel in our spiritual bodies at will, perhaps it's

possible to travel in our physical ones. As we learn more about traveling in the spirit, I would not be surprised if credible testimonies are heard where people learned how to travel in their physical bodies at will. If there is a key to learning how to do this, I suspect that it will come when we learn to see the world through God's eyes and exercise godly wisdom. It could be that God is preventing us from doing it right now because we lack the necessary wisdom to do it in a way that would not cause us harm to ourselves or others.

Acts Chapter 12

Many modern reports of spiritual travel involve the assistance of angels, who serve as guides that help travelers reach their destinations safely. Angels have the ability to open locked doors. (Once you realize a portal is a door, this can be applied in a number of different ways.) The opening of prison doors was the main focus of the book *Regions of Captivity* by Anna Mendez Ferrell. Her technique of deliverance and emotional healing involves going into spiritual places of darkness and retrieving the imprisoned alters and fragments of human souls. The twelfth chapter of the book of Acts records a case where an angel of the Lord helped Peter escape from prison:

Peter was therefore kept in prison, but constant prayer was offered to God for him by the church. And when Herod was about to bring him out, that night Peter was sleeping, bound with two chains between two soldiers; and the guards before the door were keeping the prison. Now behold, an angel of the Lord stood by him, and a light shone in the prison; and he struck Peter on the side and raised him up, saying, "Arise quickly!" And his chains fell off his hands. Then the angel said to him, "Gird yourself and tie on your sandals"; and so he did. And he said to him, "Put on your garment and follow me." So he went out and followed him, and did not know that what was done by the angel was real, but thought he was seeing a vision. When they were past the first and the second guard posts, they came to the iron gate that leads to the city, which opened to them of its own accord; and they went out and went down one street, and immediately the angel departed from him.

And when Peter had come to himself, he said, "Now I know for cer-
tain that the Lord has sent His angel, and has delivered me from the
hand of Herod and from all the expectation of the Jewish people."
ACTS 12:5-11

2 Corinthians Chapter 12

In his second letter to the church at Corinth, Paul described an incident of spiritual travel that happened years earlier. Although he didn't claim it as one of his own experiences, many commentators believe it was and that Paul omitted this fact out of humility:

It is doubtless not profitable for me to boast. I will come to visions
and revelations of the Lord: I know a man in Christ who fourteen
years ago—whether in the body I do not know, or whether out of
the body I do not know, God knows—such a one was caught up to
the third heaven. And I know such a man—whether in the body
or out of the body I do not know, God knows—how he was caught
up into Paradise and heard inexpressible words, which it is not
lawful for a man to utter.
2 COR 12:1-4

There are several things worth noting from this testimony. Paul stated that whether the experience was in the body or out he did not know. This is a common problem for those who travel in the spirit. Many travelers report being slightly confused as to whether their physical body remained and their spirit traveled by itself, or whether their physical body was transported with their spirit. It doesn't seem to be terribly important to know if an experience involved only the spirit or both spirit and body.

Many commentators have assumed that this event was the result of a near-death experience Paul suffered, but there is no way to know if this is true. Paul didn't reveal the context of the experience, so any attempt to attribute it to a near-death experience is conjecture. If it was not part of a near-death experience, there's no reason to believe you or I couldn't have a similar experience. Just as with the way Jesus ascended into heaven, Paul confirms that we can ascend into heaven.

The other thing worth mentioning is Paul's statement that he heard inexpressible words that are not lawful for a man to utter. Some have taken this as a prohibition against telling others what they have seen or heard during their spiritual journeys. There are two types of revelation given to us by God. One is intended to be shared with others; one is intended to be kept to ourselves. When an individual has an experience or receives revelation, they are usually told whether or not it may be shared. Apparently, the experience Paul had was allowed to be shared, even though the revelation that he received was not. A similar principle is found in the books of Daniel and Revelation. The prophet Daniel was told twice to seal up a book, but in Revelation, chapter 22, the apostle John was told not to seal the book. Whether or not we are allowed to share a particular revelation or experiences is a matter that the Lord can help us with.

Hebrews Chapter 11

One of the most important passages concerning spiritual travel is found in Hebrews chapter 11. It reveals much about spiritual travel.

> *By faith Enoch was taken away so that he did not see death, "and was not found, because God had taken him"; for before he was taken he had this testimony, that he pleased God. But without faith it is impossible to please Him, for he who comes to God must believe that He is, and that He is a rewarder of those who diligently seek Him.*
> HEB 11:5-6

First we are given an example—an Old Testament saint no less—who is spared from death because he walked closely with God. The most important principle regarding spiritual travel is this: the closer our relationship is with God, the more natural it becomes for us to travel in the spirit.

The second principle to note is that Enoch was a man of faith. His close relationship with God was a product of his faith. God has made us heirs of a supernatural kingdom. We're able to heal the sick, raise the dead, cast out demons, and prophesy, and it's all done by faith.

Traveling in the spirit is no different. Faith is the key to spiritual travel. Without faith it's not only impossible to please God—it's impossible to operate in the supernatural ways of the kingdom.

Since God is a Spirit, and as Jesus noted, those who want to worship Him must do it in the spirit, Enoch must have discovered a way to enter the spiritual realm and meet with God. If Enoch was able to do it, there is no reason why we can't. The key is spending time focusing our thoughts on God and learning His ways. When we do, His spiritual kingdom will become a tangible reality.

Revelation Chapter 1

The book of Revelation is a journal by the apostle John concerning his spiritual travels into the heavens. Its expressed purpose is to reveal more fully the glory of Jesus. The book opens with John's description of what he was doing when these experiences first began:

> *I was in the Spirit on the Lord's Day, and I heard behind me a loud voice, as of a trumpet, saying, "I am the Alpha and the Omega, the First and the Last," and, "What you see, write in a book and send it to the seven churches which are in Asia: to Ephesus, to Smyrna, to Pergamos, to Thyatira, to Sardis, to Philadelphia, and to Laodicea."*
> REV 1:10-11

John said he was "in the spirit" on the Lord's day. The phrase *in the spirit (en pneuma)* means "to become in the Spirit." It's a state in which we see and interact with beings in the spiritual world and receive revelation directly from them and from the Holy Spirit. It is, in a sense, being in a mental and spiritual state where our primary perceptions and actions have to do with things in the spiritual world, and we're momentarily unaware of what is happening in the physical one.

Anyone wishing to travel in the spirit can do so by learning from John's example. When we focus our attention on the spiritual realm, it becomes more real. The more often we do it, the more real it becomes and the easier it becomes to engage the realm of heaven.

Luke Chapter 24

Few of us would think that ascending into heaven is something we ought to do. But if you hope to travel in the spirit, one of the first things you must learn is to ascend into heaven. In this, as in all things, Jesus set the example for us. And while we don't need to physically ascend into heaven, the most common and safest way to travel in the spirit is first to ascend, in our spirit, into heaven. Once we are there, the options of where we can go are almost limitless. After He was resurrected, He ascended into heaven:

> *It came to pass, while He blessed them, that He was parted from them and carried up into heaven.*
> LK 24:51

Jesus has become many things to me. One of the most important is my role model. He said His disciples would do the works that He did and even greater works, because He was going to His Father. This means believers have not only the right, but the responsibility to learn to operate in all of His ways.

When I'm asked by people who are new to traveling in the spirit where they should go first, my answer is nearly always "Go to heaven and meet with Jesus." Many people have found that by ascending in their spirit into heaven they can meet with Him. Just about as often, they choose to meet with God the Father in a garden or in any number of other places.

This concludes our general overview of the biblical basis for traveling in the spirit. In later chapters we'll continue our study, discussing in more detail some of the topics we've covered.

CHAPTER THREE

The Purpose for Traveling in the Spirit

IN THIS CHAPTER WE'LL LOOK at some of the different purposes for traveling in the spirit. These are not the only purposes, but a few of the more important ones to be aware of.

Healing and Deliverance

One of the most common ways in which I experience spiritual travel is when I'm praying for healing or deliverance over distances. I receive prayer requests from around the world and because I can't physically be in the same room with the one who needs healing or deliverance, I often travel there in the spirit while praying. The curious thing is that in most cases, I'm not aware that I traveled somewhere, until someone tells me about it. As I pray for someone to be healed, I usually sit in my chair at my computer and close my eyes. As I pray, I'll often see the figure of a person appear in front of me, in my mind. Sometimes I can see myself extend my hands toward them. I pray as I'm led and then go on to the next prayer request. There isn't much in this process that would make you think it involves spiritual travel except that in some cases, I'll hear back from the person I prayed for and they'll ask if I came to visit them.

Not long ago, a friend sent me a message asking if I would pray for his friend who had a headache. I agreed to and a few minutes later, prayed as described above. About 15 minutes later, my friend sent me a message asking if I prayed for his friend. I told him I had. He then said his friend sent him a message saying that a strange man appeared in his room and stood over him with his arms outstretched, like he was praying for him. Apparently I had traveled there in the spirit, though I was not aware of it at the time.

One day I received a request from a friend who needed deliverance from a demon. She lived in another state, so I closed my eyes and in my mind, I saw my friend standing in front of me. We kept in contact by text message, so that I could check on the progress we were making. Speaking aloud, I commanded the demon to leave several times and after a few minutes she could feel it leaving. Afterward she felt much more freedom. This kind of thing happens often enough that I don't consider it unusual any more. It's just the way in which our spirit functions when it needs to accomplish certain things.

Establishing God's Government

Before He was crucified, Jesus met with His disciples and taught them how to pray. The main point of His instruction was that they should pray that the will of the Father would be done on earth in the same way it was done in heaven—that things here on earth would become a reflection of the things in heaven. The will of God is simply for heaven's reality to become earth's reality. This is one of the foundational purposes for traveling in the spirit. When God created Adam and Eve He gave them dominion over the earth. As they met with Him, they would have discovered many things about Him. They would have learned that He was their Father, but also that He is a Judge, a creative artist, and a King. And as King, He is the governmental ruler of the universe. The administration of God's governmental rule is illustrated throughout the Bible:

> *For unto us a Child is born,*
> *Unto us a Son is given;*
> *And the government will be upon His shoulder.*
> *And His name will be called*
> *Wonderful, Counselor, Mighty God,*
> *Everlasting Father, Prince of Peace.*
> *Of the increase of His government and peace*
> *There will be no end,*
> ISA 9:6-7

Throughout history, the Jews looked forward to the coming of the Messiah. Part of their hope rested in their understanding that He would come and establish a government of righteousness and overthrow the corrupt human governments typified by those of Greece and Rome. One thing the disciples didn't understand was that Jesus seemed to care little about the Roman Empire. Many refused to believe He was the Messiah because He did nothing to challenge the power of Rome.

Some believe that in a future age (the kingdom age to come) He will subdue the governments of the world and establish His righteous rule. That is one possible scenario, but there are others. It's equally possible—and I would argue this is what the New Testament bears witness to—that Jesus intended for *us* to rule and reign as His representatives. I believe one of the mandates we've been given is to establish His rule of righteousness in the earth today. God always intended to use man as His proxy—even to the point of incarnating Himself as a man to provide for us a way of salvation. As His ambassadors, it is our duty to advance His righteous rule in our own spheres of influence.

Adam and Eve were commissioned to export the culture and government of heaven to earth. It was then and is still today God's desire to colonize earth—to have His governmental rule established here. The best way to make the realities of heaven the realities of earth is to visit heaven to see its realities firsthand, and then bring them here.

Thus, one purpose for traveling to heaven is to help us function as God's representatives here on earth.

Jesus is our example of what this looks like. He said He only did what He saw the Father doing. And how exactly did He see what the Father was doing? By being there in His spirit, while He was simultaneously here on earth. His spirit communed with the Father while His body was here. He described this exact experience:

> *"No one has ascended to heaven but He who came down from heaven, that is, the Son of Man **who is in heaven**."*
> JN 3:13

He revealed that He was continually present in heaven, while at the same time being present on earth. After telling His disciples He would be betrayed by one of them, He told them He was about to go away. He revealed a little about where He was going:

> *"Let not your heart be troubled; you believe in God, believe also in Me. In My Father's house are many mansions; if it were not so, I would have told you. I go to prepare a place for you. And if I go and prepare a place for you, I will come again and receive you to Myself; that where I am, there you may be also. And where I go you know, and the way you know."*
>
> *Thomas said to Him, 'Lord, we do not know where You are going, and how can we know the way?'*
>
> *Jesus said to him, 'I am the way, the truth, and the life. No one comes to the Father except through Me.'"*
> JN 14:1-6

In this exchange, Jesus gave the disciples an invitation to go to the same place He was going. He was about to open a door, a portal if you will, through which they would have access to heaven and to the Father. As He would later reveal, He is Himself, the door. He is the portal to the throne room—the ladder that reaches into the heavens. While this passage is usually thought to refer to our access to heaven *after* our physical bodies die, the tone used here indicates that the invitation was to an immediate experience of the heavenly realms. He was inviting the disciples to encounter the Father in the same way He did—and to do it through Him. This is how we can most effectively operate as God's ambassadors. We must learn to be simultaneously in heaven and here on earth.

Our Divine Destiny

One of the purposes for traveling in the spirit is to help us discover our divine destiny. I'd like to look at a passage from the book of Jeremiah:

"Then the word of the Lord came to me, saying:
"Before I formed you in the womb I knew you;
Before you were born I sanctified you;
I ordained you a prophet to the nations."
JER 1:4-5

The Lord explained to Jeremiah that He had known him before he was conceived in his mother's womb. Many commentators have interpreted this passage as one that speaks of God's omniscience. They believe it speaks of God knowing in eternity the man Jeremiah would become after he was conceived. This is one possible explanation, but there is another, and it's one I had rejected for many years. The way this passage is constructed speaks of God knowing Jeremiah in an intimate way *before* he was conceived in his mother's womb. It speaks of God the Spirit knowing Jeremiah as a spirit before the prophet's physical body was created. After revealing this fact, the Lord continued and said that in that relationship—during Jeremiah's pre-existence in the heavenly realms, before coming to earth—God commissioned him. Before he was born, there was a heavenly ceremony in which Jeremiah was sanctified (set apart) and given a divine mandate—to be a prophet to the nations.

I once thought the idea of our pre-existence in heaven was impossible. That is, until I received one testimony after another in which people recalled in vivid detail the events that happened during their pre-existence in heaven as a spirit, before coming to earth. Let me be clear about one point: I'm not referring here to reincarnation or to previous lives people claim to have lived. The biblical narrative is clear that reincarnation is a myth. However, our pre-existence in heaven, as a spirit, before being sent to earth is a completely different matter, and it is one I believe the text of scripture supports.

It's my belief that we are created first as spirits in the heart of God. At some point after our creation, we are sent to earth to inhabit a physical body for a period of time to accomplish certain tasks and to grow spiritually, until our physical body dies. One view holds that our spirit "returns" to the heavenly realm from which it came if we've put our faith in Jesus. This view teaches that during our time on earth, we are not allowed access to heaven. It is only after our physical body dies that we can once again enter heaven. This would make accomplishing our tasks difficult, as we may not know what they are.

Another view is that after our spirit is attached to a physical body, it is still able to visit heaven and communicate with its inhabitants. Once created, our spirit is never really separated from the spiritual realm. It only seems that way. Some take the view that the experiences we may have between our physical birth and physical death are limited to experiences we can have in the earth realm. But the Bible doesn't support this view. That's actually the view endorsed by scientific naturalism. The Apostle Paul reminded believers that their citizenship was in heaven. Peter wrote that we are foreigners here, merely sojourners passing through, on our way to greater destination—our heavenly home.

It's my belief that as a spirit, we are always eternally having experiences in the realm of the spirit, including encounters with the cloud of witnesses. Rather than thinking we need to somehow activate our spirit to begin having these experiences, I believe we simply need to become more aware of the ones we're already having.

Jeremiah was commissioned by God to be a prophet to the nations before he was formed in the womb. Like him, each of us has been commissioned to accomplish certain things during our time on earth. One of the purposes for traveling in the spirit is to visit heaven to find out what we once knew. We need to know the purpose for which we were created. We need to know what mandates we've been given by God, so that we're able to accomplish them before our time here on earth is up.

From the beginning, it was God's desire to have an active, vital relationship with us. Prior to the fall, He had daily, continual fellowship with Adam and Eve. That was, and still is, His greatest desire. It's easy to think that because so many of us feel disconnected from God that His desire is to remain hidden. But nothing could be further from the truth. When Adam and Eve disobeyed God, the Lord didn't hide; Adam and Eve did. And the Father sought them out, but they withdrew from Him. Like them, many of us are still playing hide and seek from our heavenly Father.

If we perceive there is a separation between us and God, it is not because He's trying to remain hidden from us. It's because we tend to be so focused on the things of the physical world, we seldom consider what's happening in the spiritual one. And it's the spiritual realm that we must learn to tune in to if we want to communicate with Him. He has done all that is necessary on His end. We are the ones who must draw near to Him in the spiritual world.

Mitigating Disaster

There are a number of purposes for traveling in the spirit. We're only beginning to understand what they are. One purpose was revealed to me unexpectedly. Throughout the book I'll refer to a meeting called *The Gathering,* which was held in Tacoma, Washington. *The Gathering* was a meeting where I led a roundtable discussion on various subjects. During my message on traveling in the spirit, I allowed the audience to ask questions and share their experiences. One man shared the following testimony:

We were living in Missouri, around the time when the tsunami hit the coast of Japan that caused damage to the Fukushima nuclear reactor. I was in my bedroom praying, when I was suddenly taken in the spirit to Japan and I was inside the nuclear facility. While I was there, I saw a number of people in white lab coats. These were the scientists who worked there. I could see they were very focused on trying to get things under control. Even though I didn't know anything about nuclear reactors, I understood why I was there. My presence there was helping to bring stability to the reactor. As I was leaving the building I saw a number of white birds flying down into the building then flying out again. So I asked, "Father, what are these white birds?" He replied, "I have prepared teams of people that will travel like you have just done, when crisis hits in the future."

One of the purposes for traveling in the spirit seems to be to mitigate disasters. It's possible that there will be an event (or perhaps several) in the future, which will make interstate and international travel difficult or impossible. Perhaps God is preparing us now, so that when such a disaster happens, we will be able to travel anywhere He needs us without difficulty.

God is a spirit. Those who wish to know Him can only know Him as one spirit knows another. We must relate to Him in the spiritual dimension through our own spirit. Jesus said to the Samaritan woman, "The day is coming and now is when those who desire to worship God will worship Him in spirit and in truth..." (see Jn 4:23). The debate she had with the Lord was over what location was best to meet with God. The physical location on earth wasn't the issue. It was an issue of which realm was appropriate—the physical one or the spiritual one.

Waging Heavenly Warfare

Many have found Paul's letter to the church in Ephesus (particularly the sixth chapter) to be something like a blueprint for conducting spiritual warfare. In many places, he reminded the church that their rightful place was in the heavens. He taught that:
- Those who are in Christ have been blessed with all spiritual blessings in the heavenly places. (Eph 1:3)
- God made us alive together with Christ and has seated us with Him in the heavenly places. (Eph 2:5-6) NASB
- The wisdom of God is manifested *by* the church *to* the principalities and powers in the heavenly places. (Eph 3:10)
- We wage war against all the various powers of darkness in the heavenly places. (Eph 6:12)

The Bible refers to the land God promised the Israelites as *the Rest* (see Deut. 12:9). It had cities they lived in which others built. It had houses filled with good things which they did not work to acquire. It had wells which they did not dig, olive groves and vineyards which they did not plant, yet they were allowed to eat the fruit of them (see Deut. 6:10-11, Jos 24:13). It was a place prepared for them by God and they did not have to labor for any of it. But they did have to fight for it. They had to fight, but not by their own might, and not using their own strategies. They had to obey God and follow His strategies, which in the eyes of man, often seemed foolish. When the Israelites obeyed Him, they were assured victory. The only defeat they ever suffered was when they disobeyed.

This is a picture of *the rest* God wants us to enter into. This rest is not inactivity, apathy, or spiritual laziness. Rest is a mindset; a position one adopts toward their life with God. The Israelites knew they simply needed to show up for a battle and God would give them victory. They didn't need to strive to impress Him or behave like savages to intimidate their enemies. As long as they knew God was on their side and as long as they trusted in His promises, defeat was something they never worried about. In the same way, our rest is living day to day not striving to please God or trying to impress others. It's being aware that He is on our side and that He enjoys being our companion and Father. It's living without stress, anxiety, or worry, despite the fact that there are battles to be fought. The key to having victory over the powers of darkness is to wage our warfare from a place of rest and from our place in the heavens. When we engage the enemy in our own strength and when we use our own strategies, we have little hope of winning. But when we fight from where we've been given all spiritual blessings, where we've been equipped with heaven's weapons, when we fight from our rightful place—the place of rest, we will always be victorious.

Opposing Suffering and Evil

Another purpose for traveling is the spirit is to oppose suffering and evil. This is not a purpose that is always obvious at first, so we need to look at the dynamics of evil, suffering, and God's will.

It is unfortunate that so many people—even many Christians—believe that God is indifferent to the pain and suffering we go through. After all, if God is all-powerful and if He opposes evil and suffering, then why does He allow them to happen? It seems only logical that if He allows evil and suffering to happen, He must approve of them. And if He approves of them then He cannot be good. This line of reasoning is the conclusion one must come to if they believe that God is in control of everything—if everything which happens, whether good or evil, is His will.

The idea that suffering and evil are the will of God is an ancient philosophy that was given new life during the Protestant reformation. Drawing on a few passages from the scriptures such as Romans chapter nine, men like John Calvin developed a view of God that had Him in control of everything. Romans chapter nine states that God has predestined some to be saved and others to be objects of wrath. This chapter essentially teaches that all the outcomes of life are predetermined by God and we cannot change any of them. It completely ignores the fact that we have a responsibility to exercise free will.

The Bible views life from two perspectives—ours and God's. When the Bible says, "I have set before you life and death, blessing and cursing; therefore choose life," it is obviously speaking from man's perspective. It demonstrates the inescapable fact that we have free will. Romans chapter nine, which sees God in control of our choices, views life from His perspective.

The view that God is in control is a valid perspective to live from, but only if you happen to be God, and you're omniscient. If you are omniscient, you know the outcome of every person's choice. While I can accept the fact that God's perspective is valid for Him, I can't view life from an omniscient perspective if I do not know all things. Since I'm not God and I don't know who will be saved or healed, I must operate from the limited perspective of a mere human. I must live from the reality that I have free will and that I have real choices to make in my life.

One of the major stumbling blocks to traveling in the spirit is the question of whether or not God must be in control of it. It's easy to understand that we must exercise our free will when we heal the sick, give a prophetic word, or cast out a demon. Although the power of

God accomplishes these things, it is up to us to exercise our free will and do them. When it comes to traveling in the spirit, many of us don't like the idea of exercising our free will. We would prefer that God be in control of it.

Traveling in the spirit allows us to accomplish certain things and because of that, we can think of it as a tool. The thing that is produced by the use of a tool is determined by the wisdom and skill of the one using it. A hammer can be used to kill or it can be used to build a hospital or create a work of art. Like any other spiritual tool we must become proficient at traveling in the spirit in order to accomplish the things God needs us to do. If we can become proficient in using this tool, there is no reason to fear it or think God must always be in control of it. Now let's look at how God opposes evil and suffering and how He uses traveling in the spirit to do it:

The fact that God allows evil and suffering to exist doesn't mean He is not actively opposing them. It's just that He cannot force us to refrain from doing evil without removing our free will. He won't force an abusive father to stop beating his son. If He did, He would remove the man's ability to choose and negate his free will. So He must oppose evil and suffering in another way. Rather than directly negating the free will of those who want to do violence, He opposes them by recruiting those who are willing to exercise their free will to accomplish His divine purpose.

By bringing healing to those who suffer illness and injury, deliverance to those who are tormented by demons and interceding for those who suffer violence, we are God's hands that do the work which accomplishes His will. If we refuse to partner with Him, *we* are to blame for the continuation of suffering and violence.

At *The Gathering* in Tacoma, a man told me of an experience he had one night where he was taken in the spirit to a place in the heavens where he met six other people. Gauging by how they were dressed, he had to assume the others had come from different time periods spanning thousands of years, including one person who looked as if he had come from the future. They had all been brought there to pray for a boy who was being beaten by his father. The group spent time praying for the boy and when their prayer time was done, they departed. The man then found himself back in his bedroom.

Many people today assume that because suffering and violence are so widespread, God doesn't care about them. But that is simply not true. He is so interested in opposing evil and suffering that He'll find people scattered over different parts of the globe, living in different time periods, and bring them together in one place in eternity, to pray in agreement for one boy to be spared the beatings of an abusive father. This is a wonderful example of how traveling in the spirit can be used to oppose violence. If you've ever thought God doesn't care about your pain and suffering know this—He loves you enough to do the same for you.

CHAPTER FOUR

The Spiritual World

IN ORDER TO UNDERSTAND HOW we travel in the spirit, and how our mind perceives such experiences, it will help if we discuss the nature of the spiritual world and the mechanics of the human soul and spirit. I'll begin by sharing some of the most common theories of how the spiritual realms are constructed and how we experience them. You might consider this chapter to be a roadmap to follow on our travels, and a look under the hood of the human body, spirit, and soul.

Theories of the Spiritual World

The nature of the spiritual world is the subject of some debate. Even among Christians who read the same Bible, there is no universally accepted model of the heavens or the spiritual world. Some hold to a simple model that has three heavenly realms. The first being the physical skies above us, the second being the spiritual realm which is inhabited by Satan and his minions, and the third being the highest one; the realm reserved for God, His angels, and the saints.

The few Christian leaders who are pioneering spiritual travel today generally embrace a view of the spiritual world that is a bit more complex. Their models typically have one plane of existence for inhabitants of the earth, several realms of darkness that are reserved for evil spirits, and three or four heavenly realms, where God, the saints, and the angels reside.

Those in the New Age likewise endorse a more complex model of the universe which has (depending on the author) somewhere between five and seven planes of existence. It is their belief that humans possess a body which corresponds to each of these planes. They identify one of these planes as the "astral" plane. When one travels out-of-body, they would say they projected their astral body into the astral plane.

Experiencing the Spiritual World

I've read accounts from individuals who say they have also traveled out-of-body into the other planes. Those who have these experiences report a unique set of capabilities and sensations that are associated with each plane of existence. The problem is that there is no way to objectively verify any of this. There are many theories, but precious little proof to validate any of them. To further complicate the picture, scientists are convinced there are dozens or perhaps hundreds of planes of existence. But again, objective evidence that conclusively proves these theories to be true is hard to find.

I believe you can successfully travel in the spirit by using any of these models. Your ability to travel is not limited by the fact that you don't have an accurate blueprint of the spiritual universe. If successful travel depended on having one, none of us would be able to do it. If you're not sure which view of our existence is the most accurate, you might find an answer in the testimony of my friend Terry Mingus. Terry struggled with severe lung disease for years. One day he was admitted to the hospital and his condition rapidly deteriorated. While on the verge of death he had a most unusual experience. Here is his account of that experience:

I've never had an experience like this nor have I ever thought of seeing or describing things from three points of view at once, so bear with me if things get a little disjointed... they were.

Like many times before, I went in to the hospital with acute bronchitis on the verge of full-blown pneumonia. I'd been fighting to breathe for three days and my body had reached a point of complete exhaustion. I had no fight left in me. Watching my beautiful wife worry over me and fret over whether I was getting proper care and that my illness was being taken seriously pained me, as it always does. Eventually, the severity of my inability to breathe became apparent and I was admitted. I was put on a machine called a bi-pap machine—a less invasive form of a respirator—to assist my tired lungs and chest muscles to breathe. Even with the assistance of the machine, breathing was difficult and by 4 am the following morning I went into pulmonary distress. My thoracic muscles just couldn't handle the work load of breathing anymore. I was not getting enough oxygen and my body began to shut down.

I remember waking up struggling to get a breath of air. The machine seemed to be working against me and, in a panic, I grabbed the respirator mask and tore it off my face. I grabbed the call button and hit the emergency button. Though I am sure it was only a moment, it seemed like forever before I got a response. The nursing staff tried to calm me down and adjust the machine to help me breathe. But I was beyond having time to calm down. I needed air now! I heard one of the staff say, "This isn't good. He's in distress, call the head of ICU." I was too busy trying to get air, so I tore off the mask and with the last bit of strength I had, I ran for the hospital room door where I ran into a nurse who grabbed me and told me I need to get back in the bed. My response was to use the last air in my lungs to gasp as loud as I could, "I can't breathe!"

I was standing in the door speaking to the nurse, explaining that I could not breathe, but I was also seeing this whole scene from a slightly elevated place at the same time. As if this weren't strange enough, as the nurse and an aide grabbed me and led me back to the bed and sat me down, I was aware that I was still standing in the doorway of the room—and in the elevated point of view—being in all three places at the same time.

Sitting on the bed, I could hear the concerned staff discussing who needed to be called: my wife, my doctor, the head of ICU, and to bring in a crash cart because I was crashing as they spoke. My lungs were exhausted and just stopped trying to pull in air. I was losing control of my body and saying, "Ok Father, I am in your hands now," even though I knew I was dying and was terrified. Standing in the doorway, I could see and hear all of this going on, including those inner thoughts that I sent to God. I was frozen in the doorway unable to move.

The doorway was brightly lit with a golden-red light to my left which flowed right through me. My left arm and leg were on the outside of the doorway, which now no longer led to the hospital hallway, but to a vast, open space from which the light of eternity was visible. My right arm and leg were on the inside of the door. The light and energy I saw to my left was flowing from outside the room through my left side, out of my right side and then into the part of me who was sitting on the bed. From the third elevated point of view, I witnessed all of those things occurring as well. I observed the scene from three different points of view at the same time—even sharing the inner thoughts of each perspective.

At this point, I was pretty terrified. As a matter of fact, all three of me were terrified.

What was going on?

Why was I experiencing this in three separate ways simultaneously?

Was I dying?

Then I heard that sweet, still, small voice that has been my constant companion all my life. I knew this voice intimately. It was with me even before I was living for God. He asked me, "Is this it for you? Is this really all you wanted out of the life you were given? Are you really satisfied with the way things are? Are you really ready to quit?"

I heard this from all three places—the doorway, the bed, and the elevated viewpoint. Suddenly, it set in what was going on. I was suspended between life and death and meeting with my Father. There was no anger in his voice. As a matter of fact, it was the same loving voice that had always helped me and encouraged me when disaster entered my life. The same voice that had talked me through weighing and measuring right and wrong, good and evil, this direction in life or that. I wish all the thoughts, all the things exchanged in that meeting could be put into words, but it really isn't possible. Images of life events, people who I had hurt or helped. Things I had done and things I had always meant to do, but never seemed to find the time. Hours seemed to pass in a few seconds or maybe it was seconds passing that seemed like hours.

All the time while I was sitting on the bed, I was hearing all of this and saw myself in the doorway with my arms outstretched like I was hanging in midair. Looking much like the images of people hanging on crosses, with the red light flowing through me. I was aware of the third me sitting slightly above us experiencing all of this too. All of us were separate, and yet one.

I was watching the nurses putting the mask on my face again forcing air into me. The crash cart rolled in. The head of the ICU walked in the door with the nursing supervisor of the hospital. They were all trying to figure out what my body was going to do. I was sitting up in total rigidity. My arms suddenly jerked back in a most unnatural posture like a pole had been slid between my bent arm and my back. There was something else there... something trying to accelerate the dying process. It was phantom-like and silent and it was hurting me.

Suddenly, every fiber of my body was wracked with excruciating pain. I was no longer breathing. From the doorway, I watched them lay my body back on the bed and pull the hospital gown away. They applied jell to two spots on my chest and torso and started the defibrillator charging. My Fathers voice said, "The choice is yours. It always has been. It always will be your choice. What do you want, Terry?"

I replied from the third spot elevated above the room, "I want to live. I am needed and there are things you put in my heart that are left undone. But Father if that is not your will, I am okay with not staying. If you want me to go, I will go. If you want me to stay, I will stay... I surrender."

"So be it," He softly answered.

Suddenly, the golden-red light swelled. The me that was standing in the door felt my skin flutter like being in a high-velocity vehicle when the g-force reaches a certain level. The light shot from my right hand into the me that was on the bed and suddenly I was on the bed breathing and the nurse said, "Wait he's ok now, he's breathing… heart beat is steady. That was scary."

I personally hold to the traditional three-fold view of man which says we are a spirit, possessing a soul, inhabiting a physical body. I'm even more convinced of this after hearing Terry's testimony.

The following sections provide information about the nature of the spiritual body and the spiritual world. I've included a brief look at how we communicate in the spiritual world, how our soul relates to our spirit, and how our imagination is used to receive information from the spiritual world. This information may not seem important now, but it serves as a foundation for material we'll cover in later chapters.

The Spiritual Body

Your spiritual body is young in appearance. There are some exceptions, such as spirits who have subjected themselves to darkness and suffering, but most spirits have the appearance of youth and vitality. There is a translucence to the spiritual body, but it also has a surprisingly solid appearance. If you were to grab your spirit's left arm with your spirit's right hand, it would feel solid.

One difference between the physical and spiritual bodies is that the spiritual body emanates light while the physical body reflects it. Not all spiritual bodies emit the same quality of light. The spiritual condition of a being may be discerned by observing the quality of light emitted from its body. Angels of God typically emit brilliant light of various colors. Demons often appear as spirits that are composed of darkness and shadows.

Spiritual Communication

Communication in the spiritual world is done directly from spirit to spirit through the transmission of thought impressions and visual imagery. This communication bypasses the physical structures of the human body that we normally use to communicate, such as our mouths and eardrums. Spiritual communication does not use language. In the spirit, one can understand all of the thoughts of anyone from any culture, regardless of their native language. This understanding is possible because spiritual thoughts transcend human language. Concepts and emotions are communicated telepathically.

When God speaks to you, He doesn't speak in human language even though it seems as though He does. Your spirit receives impressions which are interpreted by your soul in the language you're familiar with. Some of the concepts that your spirit understands cannot be translated into human language as there are no words to adequately express them. In the spirit, there is a direct impartation of experience and knowledge that is unlike anything in the physical world. One instantly "knows" what is being communicated in the deepest, most complete way.

Thoughts

All spirits emanate spiritual light through their thoughts. This light reveals the various strengths and weaknesses of the spirit. Thoughts in the spiritual realm also have creative power. For example, creative miracles of healing are done in the spiritual world through thoughts. If you imagine a broken bone being mended, it will be mended. Where you go and what you do in the spiritual realm is also generally determined by your thoughts. This is something to consider carefully. Because the direction and destination of our spiritual travel is usually determined by our thoughts, we must learn to bring our thought life under control, or we may go places we don't intend to go and see things we don't wish to see.

The Soul

Our spirit is what links us consciously to God and the rest of the spiritual world. Our body is what links us to the physical world, and our soul is the connector between them. It is the meeting place and communication juncture between the physical and spiritual worlds. The soul is able to perceive the spiritual world as easily as it perceives the physical one. Whichever world the soul is focused on, that is the one we are most aware of, (what we are conscious of) and it's the one we perceive to be the most real.

The human brain continually processes input from the physical senses of touch, taste, sight, smell, and sound. What you may not realize is that your spirit has all the same senses that your physical body has. As your spirit receives sensory input from the spiritual world, it relays the information to your soul. But because experiences in the spiritual world are so different from those in the physical one, you may have little ability to make sense of them. The fantastic imagery and strange messages coming from the spiritual world can be so bizarre and fleeting that they're often thought to come from our imagination. This is why messages from God, demons, and angels are often interpreted as our own thoughts.

The Imagination

When we speak about our imagination, many of us think back to our childhood and the imaginary friends we had, the stories we made up, or the games we played to amuse ourselves. Children find it easy to engage the imaginary realm. As we grow older, we're taught that the imaginary realm is one of foolishness and make-believe. The phrase, "it's just your imagination," is used to dismiss the inspired ideas that come from this part of the soul, and downgrade the importance of the spiritual feedback we may be receiving. Of course the dismissal was not intended to be harmful; adults were doing what they thought was best. Focus on what is "really" here. It's this mindset that drove most of us to focus more on the physical realm than the spiritual one.

In Genesis 8:21 the Lord said, "I will never again curse the ground for man's sake, although the imagination of man's heart is evil from his youth." In this verse, the Lord identifies the location of the imagination. It resides in the "heart" of man.

The Hebrew word *leb*, translated "heart" does not refer to the physical heart, but the "inner man," or what we commonly call the soul. Some take this comment from God to mean that the human imagination is incapable of anything but evil. They believe we must resist any influence that comes from our imagination. But there is another way in which this verse can be interpreted.

Your imagination can be used to create things of beauty as well as things that are hideous. It is capable of creating both the sublime and the profane—that which is good and that which is evil. Because we have free will, we are capable of choosing what we create in our imagination. The passage in question simply states that prior to the flood, people chose to exercise their free will for evil purposes. They preferred to entertain evil in their imagination rather than good.

Man is made in the image of God, who describes Himself as a Creator. Because we are created in His image, we've been given similar creative abilities. And we are most like Him when engaged in the act of creation ourselves.

Our spirit is our creative center. When we speak and act from our spirit, we're able to call things into existence that did not exist previously, the same way God does. If you were to pray for someone who needed a new kidney, your spirit could cause a new one to come into existence. That is the creative power of our spirit. The spirit is also the place where original creative ideas are formed, and where creative inspiration is received from outside sources, such as angels and the Holy Spirit. This information is then relayed to our soul to be interpreted by our imagination. My wife often receives inspiration for paintings through dreams and visions that she receives in her spirit. I receive inspiration for books in the same way.

Our imagination is the place in our soul where we visualize what it is we need or want our spirit to create. God created the imagination as a way for our soul to receive spiritual insights and His divine plans and purposes. Once an idea or concept is transferred from our spirit to our soul, via the imagination, it can be processed by our brain and acted upon. Allow me to illustrate what this looks like:

When the Lord gave Noah instructions for building an ark, it seems likely that He may have revealed the dimensions of the ark, the materials to be used, and the process of constructing it through Noah's imagination.

When He gave Moses details about the construction of the tabernacle, He wanted it to be a replica of things in heaven. Since Moses had limited information to work with, it seems likely that the information that was imparted came through his imagination. And when the artisans and craftsmen were asked to create ornamental items for the tabernacle, the details were probably given to them through their imaginations.

Revelation from both heavenly and demonic beings is received the same way—through the imagination. In addition to the beautiful scenes we're shown from heaven, the imagination stores the grotesque, the perverted, and the frightening images we've been exposed to. We may have experienced spiritual travel into dark places when we were children, and these images are often stored in this part of our soul. The kingdom of darkness bombards our imagination with unpleasant images to harass, intimidate, and enslave us. The goal of the enemy is to so pollute the flow of revelation we receive through it that we'll decide we don't want to see anything at all. But God wants to reveal His kingdom to us through it, too. Because it is part of the soul, and the soul is controlled by our will, we can willingly choose to do whatever we want with our imagination. And because much of the imagery we receive from the enemy is painful, in order to avoid the pain associated with these images, some of us have exercised our free will and chosen to completely shut down the flow of revelation that comes through it. In an attempt to safeguard our soul from the enemy's attacks, we've unknowingly blocked our ability to receive revelation from God. If we exercise our free will and make the conscious choice to receive revelation again through our imagination, our "spiritual eyes" will again be opened and we'll be able to see and travel in the spirit. The solution is not to avoid receiving all of the imagery that comes through our imagination, but to filter it. This is done by rejecting evil thoughts and images and focusing only on those which are positive. This process is sometimes called *sanctifying* or setting it apart for God's purposes.

Visions

It is not essential to see visions before one can travel in the spirit, but being able to see them does offer some benefit. When I use the term "vision" I'm using a simple term which actually describes a number of different experiences. As I use the term, I'm referring to our ability to see something in the spiritual world that we would not be able to see with our physical eyes alone. What most often happens when we see a vision is that our spirit perceives something in the spiritual world and that information is transferred to our brain which our soul perceives as an image in our mind.

Visions are accessible to everyone, even if we believe we have never seen one. Because some individuals are adept at seeing them while others are not, there are some who have suggested that seeing visions is a gift that is given only to a few people. This teaching is widespread, but is neither biblical, nor is it the experience of those who successfully see visions.

Every human spirit has a healthy pair of spiritual eyes. Even if we are not consciously aware that our spirit is seeing things in the spiritual world, our spiritual eyes always perceive things in that world. The problem is that the information our spirit receives is relayed to our brain, but processed at the subconscious level instead of the conscious one. We receive it, but aren't *aware* of it. The information is available to us, but our conscious awareness is generally focused on what we see in the physical world. Seeing (perhaps *recognizing* is a better word) in the spiritual world comes when we change our focus, or our *awareness,* from what we see in the physical world to what we see in the spiritual one. The key to perceiving and understanding spiritual communication is having our spiritual senses trained and refocused on the spiritual world. (I have more teaching on this subject in my book *Seeing in the Spirit Made Simple.*)

One of the most common misunderstandings about visions is the idea that they are external to us. Sometimes a vision may appear to be external, but most times it will appear in the same way any other visual image appears in our mind—through our imagination. And there has been much confusion over this among both Christians and non-Christians.

We use the same apparatus to see an angel standing in front of us that we use to imagine what our husband or wife may be doing at work. We've been taught by society (programmed really) to think that anything which we see in our imagination is not real. Glimpses of spiritual things find their way into our imagination continually. Our spirit attempts to relay them to our brain through our imagination. But we've been trained to ignore them, so we dismiss the appearance of spiritual beings and divine revelation as being "just our imagination."

Most people who see visions are not born with the ability fully developed. They learn to see them over time with exercise and practice. That's how I developed my spiritual vision. When I began learning to see visions, I set time aside every day to practice seeing in the spirit. I spent hours lying down with my eyes closed, and I asked God to show me what He wanted me to see. At first, the images I saw in my mind were blurry. But during the weeks and months that I did these exercises, my spiritual vision became quite clear, and today, I can generally see more clearly in the spiritual world than I can in the physical one.

I'd like to share one of my earliest spiritual travel testimonies:

One afternoon, I relaxed in a chair and began telling God I didn't want to see anything of the earth, but only things of heaven. I repeated this over and over with my eyes closed. I saw in my mind a man who looked like Moses standing on a cloud-covered mountain top. Then I saw a group of people in heaven, who all looked very much alike, standing with their arms outstretched. They had their arms raised and they began singing. All around them was a beautiful illumination of piercing, brilliant light. Then I began to see drops of liquid light flying around. The drops of light seemed to be showers that were coming from the throne of God. Then the vision changed and I saw a crown that looked something like the crown of thorns, but it was made up of strands of interwoven, white light. There were projections coming from it pointing upward like thorns, but they were made of pure white fibers that had their own illumination. The crown was massive. I could not estimate its size. Below the crown, I saw nothing but a brilliant light of purest white. I looked at this image for a while and then the vision faded away.

To one who is not acquainted with spiritual travel, this might seem like nothing more than the workings of my imagination. But I believe it was much more than that. This is actually the most common way in which our spirit travels. Our physical body remains where it is. Our spirit visits some heavenly place and reports back what it sees by projecting onto the little TV screen in our mind what it is observing. In most cases, traveling in the spirit is no more complicated than that.

Exercise

In my book on seeing in the spirit, I included an exercise that has proven to be helpful not just in assisting readers to see in the spiritual realm, but to obtain healing from the emotional trauma of their past. Because so many readers found it beneficial, I'm including the same exercise in this chapter.

Some people have traveled in the spirit or read about it and found it to be frightening or dangerous. These feelings have caused them to make an inner vow never to be involved in it again. These vows have power and they often prevent the ones who made them from being able to see or travel in the spirit. If you've ever made such a vow to yourself (or anyone else) it's a good idea to renounce this vow and tell the Holy Spirit your desire to see and travel in the spirit again.

For the person who is plagued with unpleasant images when they see or travel in the spirit, it may be a good idea to begin by healing the painful emotions and traumatic memories from the past. Receiving healing of painful emotions and memories can be a fairly straight-forward process that consists of three simple steps:

1. Identifying the painful emotion associated with a particular event.

2. Asking Jesus to take the painful emotion from you.

3. Asking Him to heal the wound in your soul caused by it.

For many people, emotional healing really can be that simple. The main problem I've found is that people who are extremely rational by nature tend to ask a lot of "why" questions in the middle of the healing process, which can cause distractions and impede the healing process. While God may at some point reveal why a certain event happened to you, in the immediate setting of emotional healing, the more important question is *how* the event affected you. When you recall the event does it evoke emotions of anger or sadness? Do you feel shame, guilt or some other emotion? If you focus on the emotions you're feeling, and identify them one-by-one and allow Jesus to heal them, it's likely that you'll be able to see and travel in the spiritual realm without the fear of painful memories getting in the way. I've received healing from emotional wounds from my own childhood. I'd like to share the process I've used since then to help people receive healing. (You might ask a trusted friend to help you with this exercise or you can do it yourself.)

One of the things Jesus purchased for us on the cross is healing of our painful emotions. The Bible says that Jesus has borne our griefs and carried our sorrows (Is 53:4). If He has borne them for us then we do not need to carry them any longer.

Healing painful emotions usually requires you to go back to events in your life where you can feel an emotion that is troubling you. Once you have accessed the memory of a particular event and you feel the emotion associated with it, ask Jesus to come to you. If the emotion you're feeling is sinful, confess it as a sin and ask Him to forgive you of it. Say that you believe the blood of Jesus has taken away the penalty and consequences of your sin.

Identify the emotion you're feeling. Tell Jesus you want the emotion removed from your soul. Ask Him to heal the wound in your soul caused by the emotion. Tell Him you receive His healing.

An optional step that some people find helpful is to ask Jesus to give you something positive to replace the negative emotion that He is removing. If you ask Him to take away sadness, you might ask Him to give you joy. If you ask Him to take away anger, you might ask Him to give you peace. If the emotion is there because you believed a lie about that situation, ask Him to show you the truth about it.

When you are done with this, bring the memory of the painful event to your mind again. If the emotion was healed, you should not be able to feel it any longer, but there may be a different negative emotion that you can feel. Determine what negative emotion is strongest and do the same thing with it that you did with the first emotion. Tell Jesus you want the emotion removed from your soul. Ask Him to heal the wound in your soul caused by it and tell Him you receive His healing.

When you are done, bring the memory of the painful event to your mind again. Once more, try to determine if there are any negative emotions. If there are, repeat this process until you can bring the event to your memory and you feel no negative emotions. This process can be used on any memories that are associated with negative emotions.

CHAPTER FIVE

Speaking with the Cloud of Witnesses

I WAS RAISED IN A Catholic home. Around the age of 12, I became fed up with religion and the hypocrisy I saw in the church and stopped attending mass. In college, I loved the sciences and soon embraced Darwinian evolution. I was content to live as an atheist, but at the age of 38, I had a dramatic conversion to Christianity. After becoming a believer, I attended a non-denominational evangelical church. The pastors I learned from detested everything about Catholicism and naturally, I did as well. I especially despised the belief that it's acceptable—even desirable—to pray to or speak to saints who have passed into eternity. Like many Protestants, I haven't merely been skeptical toward the idea, but downright hostile. My hostility wasn't just rooted in teachings from my new pastors, but in the many negative experiences I'd had in the church as a child. As we turn our attention to the prohibition against "consulting with the dead" I want you to know it's a subject I take very seriously. It's also one I've been very much opposed to, until recently.

The writer of the book of Hebrews has much to say about those who have died and passed into eternity. He refers to them as "the cloud of witnesses." The eleventh chapter of Hebrews is sometimes referred to as the "hall of faith." The writer waxes eloquently about how *by faith,* the patriarchs, the prophets, and lesser-known people pleased God. The last two verses of the chapter summarize his point:

> *And all these, having obtained a good testimony through faith, did not receive the promise, God having provided something better for us, that they should not be made perfect apart from us.*
> HEB 11:39-40

The writer notes that the gathering of saints who have gone before us are not perfect, or *complete* without us. We must be joined to them in order to have a complete body. Chapter 12 begins:

> *Therefore we also, since we are surrounded by so great a cloud of witnesses...*
> HEB 12:1

The phrase in this verse, *are surrounded by,* means "to be closely joined to a person or thing." It speaks of our relationship to the cloud of witnesses. The writer says that the spirits of the departed are surrounding us and we're in the midst of them. It's not as if they are off in the distance, over there, in the past, or waiting for us to join them. It says we are *presently* among them. It describes a present, intimate relationship with the cloud of witnesses—those who have run their race well. Think of a stadium filled with friends and relatives who have gone before you. Currently, right this minute, you and I are surrounded—enclosed by a crowd of not-quite-visible saints.

If you're wondering what a *saint* is, allow me to briefly explain this term. Catholicism teaches that a follower of Jesus must accomplish a number of great things and be recognized by the Vatican in order to be a saint. Although this is a popular teaching, the New Testament, and in particular the teachings of the Apostle Paul, say otherwise. In many of his letters, Paul addressed ordinary believers as saints. Whether living in a physical body or living in eternity, any believer may be referred to as a saint.

As you may have guessed, God often speaks to me through dreams. I suspect that many times when we meet someone in a dream, it is not an image of them we are interacting with or even, as some would suggest, Jesus or the Holy Spirit, but the spirit of the actual person.

Some time ago, I ran across a rare audio recording of a message by C.S. Lewis. The message was a speech that formed the outline of what would become one of his most well-known books—*Mere Christianity*. I converted the message into a video which I posted on YouTube. I'm not a whiz at video production and the project took most of the day. During that time, my mind had become obsessed with the message of this beloved saint whose writings have inspired a generation. Lewis has inspired me more than anyone, apart from Jesus Himself. The reason he inspires me is his gift of writing. Being a writer, I gravitate toward gifted writers. I draw inspiration from them and pick up tips on writing. I learn from their examples as I hone my own skills. It's hard to think of anyone who so eloquently and so intelligently wrote about the issues that believers wrestle with. We all need role models, and over the years I've adopted Lewis as the main person by whom I gauge my own writing, and at times, my own thinking. While writing, I often wonder, how would he have addressed this issue? How would he build an argument for this point?

I never had a chance to meet him. He became a member of the great cloud of witnesses in 1963. The day I created the video, I spent an unusually long period of time wondering about him and reflecting on how his life had affected mine. Time itself seemed to stand still that afternoon, and then I went to sleep.

I had a dream that night where Lewis paid me a visit. I did not see him in the way you might typically see someone in a dream. It's not as though we were sitting at a table talking. I simply knew I was in his presence, the way you know certain facts in dreams. I also did not hear him speak the way you typically hear someone speak in a dream. I did not hear that distinctive accent. He spoke to me spirit-to-spirit through the transmission of thoughts. The purpose of our meeting was so that he could teach me a few things about writing. There I was in a dream being tutored by the spirit of one of my favorite men. And what he shared was surprisingly practical.

He told me about how the proper selection of words is critical to being a successful writer, and illustrated his point with several stories about the problems he ran into by not choosing the right words. He noted that our choice of words creates either a favorable or an unfavorable experience in the mind of the reader and that the selection of one word or another can make a huge difference in how our writing is perceived. He gave several examples of how the choice of this word or that one created a completely different set of circumstances, and told me to choose my words with care.

Some would argue that this was nothing more than the result of eating too much pizza. Some would say my mind was working out the issue I was focused on that day. Others would say it was an evil spirit masquerading as Lewis who intended to deceive me. It's possible that it was the Holy Spirit or Jesus teaching me through a persona I was familiar with. And some would say it was indeed the spirit of Lewis himself, who was granted access to me that night so that he might assist me in advancing God's plans.

Mike Parsons has been mentoring believers in living supernaturally for several decades and he's met with a number of people from the cloud of witnesses. According to him, when these saints meet with us, they tend to help those who are engaged in endeavors similar to their own calling. They usually share practical advice on how to avoid certain problems they ran into during their time on earth while involved in their own work. They tend to give suggestions about how to accomplish things with expediency and efficiency, to shorten the learning curve, so to speak. And that's exactly what Lewis did. Although I once stood opposed to anything of this nature, my meeting with Lewis and the testimonies of trustworthy leaders like Mike Parsons has caused me to rethink my position.

One of the most fascinating passages in the entire Bible is Matthew's account of the transfiguration of Jesus. Matthew describes it this way:

Now after six days Jesus took Peter, James, and John his brother, led them up on a high mountain by themselves; and He was transfigured before them. His face shone like the sun, and His clothes became as white as the light. And behold, Moses and

Elijah appeared to them, talking with Him.
MT 17:1-3

Elijah and Moses are saints of the Old Testament who had passed from the scene long ago. It's often taught that we should never attempt to have conversations with the spirits of the dead. Yet here is Jesus talking with two saints who had been dead for centuries. Some will point out that Elijah did not actually die. He was taken into heaven supernaturally in a whirlwind. But we know that Moses died. God Himself buried the body (see Deut 34:5-6). We must now ask if Jesus violated the prohibition in Deuteronomy when He spoke with these saints. The Bible says Jesus lived as a man, but without sin, therefore we know it must not have been a violation of the scriptures for Him to speak with them.

There is another passage we can learn from that is found in the book of Acts. After He was raised from the dead, but before He ascended into heaven, Jesus met with the disciples, who were still unclear about His plans. They were under the impression that He was going to overthrow the Roman government and reestablish the political rule of Israel.

Therefore, when they had come together, they asked Him, saying, "Lord, will You at this time restore the kingdom to Israel?" And He said to them, "It is not for you to know times or seasons which the Father has put in His own authority. But you shall receive power when the Holy Spirit has come upon you; and you shall be witnesses to Me in Jerusalem, and in all Judea and Samaria, and to the end of the earth."

Now when He had spoken these things, while they watched, He was taken up, and a cloud received Him out of their sight. And while they looked steadfastly toward heaven as He went up, behold, two men stood by them in white apparel, who also said, "Men of Galilee, why do you stand gazing up into heaven? This same Jesus, who was taken up from you into heaven, will so come in like manner as you saw Him go into heaven."
ACTS 1:6-11

Have you ever wondered who the "men in white apparel" were who spoke to the disciples? There is no suggestion whatsoever that they were angels. The "men in white apparel" were the same type of being as those mentioned in the book of Revelation who are described as "elders" (see Rev 4:4, 7:13-14). They were the spirits of men—members of the cloud of witnesses, and they spoke to the disciples about the Lord's return. Here we have what some would call a violation of the prohibition against consulting with the spirits of the dead.

Let's look at a modern example of consulting with spirits of the dead:

In the Zulu practice of witchcraft, witch doctors understand that the spirits which give them knowledge and power are their ancestral spirits—those of their departed grandparents and great-grandparents. These spirits provide guidance and they watch over the ones who show them loyalty. My friend Alan Champkins was trained as a Zulu shaman. He learned that with ancestral spirits, you must always offer a sacrifice and be obedient if the spirits are going to take care of you. Disobey them and you risk becoming the victim of their anger. There's always a trade-off with such spirits and inevitably, you end up becoming a slave to their demands. Just before he was about to graduate into a full-fledged witch doctor, the Holy Spirit alerted Alan to the fact that these were not spirits of his ancestors, but demons that wanted to destroy him. He has since become a spirit-filled teacher of healing and deliverance.

The prohibition in Deuteronomy against consulting with spirits of the dead was not intended as a strict law against having any type of contact with the departed, or specifically with those who have joined the cloud of witnesses. It was a prohibition against contacting spirits for the purpose of fortune telling. This is because such spirits are not really ancestral spirits or even helpful ones, but demons.

Many of us seek protection or information about our future from witch doctors and psychics because we don't believe we can receive it from God. The fear that God won't reveal our future or protect us causes us to seek help from other sources. Fear is the real issue God was addressing in Deuteronomy. A heart filled with fear doesn't trust that God is able or willing to guide us and take care of us. Yet it is an unfounded fear. In the same way God revealed to Jeremiah his future and promised to watch over him, He wants to do the same for you. All you need to do is come before Him and ask.

Visitations

When a person's physical body dies, they continue to live on in the spiritual world. Though we think of them as being dead, they are still very much alive. If we happen to be visited by a recently departed loved one who wants to tell us we shouldn't worry about them, how is this evil? If the spirit of an Old Testament prophet visits us for the purpose of instructing us in prophetic ministry, how is this sinful?

I've hosted public discussions where I've asked friends to share testimonies about communicating with spirits of the departed. You might be surprised at how often this happens. The most common occurrence is a brief visit from a recently (or soon to be) departed loved one who shares a short message of hope or love to someone before moving on into eternity. In most cases this is the last contact the person has with the one who has departed. Sometimes the visitation comes in the form of the person's spirit; sometimes it's a familiar fragrance, a shaft of light, or the appearance of some other form, along with a short message.

There are times when we may be allowed to visit with a saint who has departed. These saints usually have instructions from God about how they are to assist us. In my case, C.S. Lewis had the ability (and permission from God) to help me with my divine assignment as a writer. Unfortunately, *we* seldom have access to this kind of information. Unless the spirit we're communicating with has a specific, divinely ordained purpose for the meeting, it's likely that an evil spirit may try to meet with us instead. Such encounters may seem like they are ordained by God, but they may instead be arranged by the enemy. This is why it can be dangerous for *us* to initiate such a relationship. If we initiate contact with a spirit, not knowing whether there is a divine purpose for it, we can leave ourselves open to the influence of a demon that is looking for just such an encounter.

One type of demon to be aware of is what is commonly called a familiar (or familial) spirit. These are demons that have an attraction to certain families. They tend to interact with the descendants of a particular family for many generations. They sometimes pretend to be the spirit of a departed relative. You may be visited by a familiar spirit, but they are not difficult to detect if you know what to look for.

Testing the Spirits

The agenda of a familiar spirit typically involves the creation of a lasting relationship—one that causes the individual to become dependent upon them for something. Familiar spirits may ask us to trade something with them. They typically offer some kind of knowledge or power in exchange for companionship, which over time, becomes a dependency upon them. Familiar spirits may also have (or pretend to have) extensive knowledge of our family lineage and they can become violent or threatening when told to leave. True spirits of the recently departed don't put demands on the one they visit. They tend to be concerned only with imparting joy or hope to one who may be grieving. They are not interested in developing lasting connections.

Many of us have a misconception about the spirit world, which says that every spirit is fiercely loyal either to God or to Satan, and it's our job to discern each spirit's loyalty. What we want is an easy litmus test which will forever settle the matter. Some have assumed that such a test really exists, and that it can be found in first John chapter four:

> *By this you know the Spirit of God: Every spirit that confesses that Jesus Christ has come in the flesh is of God, and every spirit that does not confess that Jesus Christ has come in the flesh is not of God...*
> 1 JN 4:2-3

Many believe we simply need to ask every spirit if Jesus came in the flesh. If the answer is no, we pull a marker from our pocket and draw a black mark on them and never believe anything they say. If they answer in the affirmative, we get their phone number and invite them over for tea. Wouldn't it be convenient if this were actually how it worked?

The question John proposed needs to be placed in its historical context. John was writing to a body of believers who had been influenced by false teachers, and in particular—a teaching known as Gnosticism. One of the gnostic teachings was that the physical world was completely corrupt and evil. The teaching went on to say that God would never inhabit a corrupt, fleshly body, because all flesh is evil. The Gnostics taught that Jesus could not have come in the flesh if He were God. He

78

must have only been a spirit or phantom if He were truly God. John's question then was addressed to anyone who had heard this teaching. If any teacher denied that Jesus came in the flesh, believers could know that the teacher was not sent from God—but teaching one of the lies of Gnosticism.

Many have taken this verse and used it to try to determine if a spirit is from God or from Satan. The problem is that we believe that the saints and angels of God can only tell the truth and fallen angels and demons can only lie. This is why we believe the litmus test works. We believe that once we identify a spirit as false, it will always be false and when one is proven to be truthful, it will always be truthful. All we need to do is make note of which is which and never confuse them. The scriptures however, portray this issue quite differently as the following two stories illustrate:

A demon-possessed woman had followed the Apostle Paul and his friends for many days, loudly proclaiming, "These men are the servants of the Most High God, who proclaim to us the way of salvation!"

Does this sound like something a demon would say? If this woman were to come into most churches today, she'd be received as a prophet. She spoke the truth, even under the influence of a demon. Yet Paul discerned the presence of a demon and cast it out of her (see Acts 16:17-18).

Isaiah was instructed by the Lord to tell King Hezekiah the sickness he had contracted was fatal. The prophet delivered the message, but a few minutes later the Lord told him to go back and tell the King he would not die after all (see 2 Kgs 20:1-6). Imagine the prophet's confusion over being told the information he had just given was wrong.

Situations like these illustrate the true nature of the spiritual world. Demons can be honest; Satan told the truth when the Lord asked where he had been. And men of God can be wrong. Every pastor you've ever had has told a few lies and every demon you've ever had has said a few honest things. There is in all of us a mixture of light and dark, and a litmus test won't reveal what we're looking for. The best way to test the spirits—to see if something is of God or not—is the same way we test anything else. Look at the fruit.

How do we judge the fruit? First, it isn't necessary to judge the messenger. We don't need to delve into the deepest recesses of their heart to measure their loyalty to God. All we need to do is ask ourselves how our time with them has affected us. Has the revelation we received from them or the experiences we've had led us closer to God, or has it gotten in the way of our relationship with Him? Has it made the Lord seem more wonderful to us, or has it made us less enthusiastic about Him? And most importantly, has it diverted our attention in any way away from Jesus and toward something else, even if that something is not evil? Allow me to illustrate what this looks like:

There is nothing wrong with getting to know your angels a little better. But as you get to know them, you should also be increasing in your knowledge of God, who is the One they represent. If any spirit (or any human) causes you to focus more on angels and meeting with them than on meeting with the Lord and getting to know Him better, you may be wise to re-evaluate exactly where this relationship is taking you.

Although a demon is able to tell the truth (as Legion did when the Lord demanded his name), what they can't do is produce the fruit of the Spirit: love, joy, peace, longsuffering, kindness, goodness, faithfulness, gentleness, and self-control. Demons and fallen angels can speak as ones who are wise and can demonstrate great power. But the more you interact with them, the more you will bear the fruit of darkness and inevitably be lured away from the true light—Jesus. Any spirit you meet who does not help you grow closer to the Lord should be considered suspect.

PART TWO
How We Travel
in the Spirit

CHAPTER SIX

Terminology for Spiritual Travel

FOR THE SAKE OF CLARITY, I'd like to provide a few definitions for the terms I'll use in the following chapters and an explanation of why I've chosen them.

James Maloney has previously written on this subject in his series *Ladies of Gold: The Remarkable Ministry of the Golden Candlestick*. When speaking of how we travel into the heavens, Maloney uses the word "rapture." Because many people associate "rapture" with a different experience, I've decided not to use that term. When Maloney writes about a person who is permanently taken into heaven without their body undergoing physical death, he uses the term "translation." Although this is consistent with the way this word is used to describe how Enoch was taken to live with God in heaven, we have no such testimonies to report in this book. When Maloney describes a person being physically transported in their body, supernaturally, he uses the word "transport."

I have no objections to the terms Maloney has used in his books. They're simply the words that the women of the Golden Candlestick used. We must however, consider the fact that his books report on spiritual travel, but don't teach readers how to do it. Because they are not instructional, they don't contain an instructional vocabulary. Other authors have written instructional books and it seems like their vocabulary may be better suited for our purposes.

Bruce Allen wrote a book on spiritual travel titled *Gazing into the Glory*. He has since taught extensively on this subject. In doing so, he established an instructional vocabulary. Michael Van Vlymen has also written instructional books and has used the same terms Bruce used. I believe it's important to maintain a consistent dialogue, so I've chosen to use the same terms and definitions Bruce and Michael have used.

I consider *translation* or *translation by faith* to be when our spirit travels somewhere while our physical body remains unaffected.

A *trance* is similar to translation, but in a trance, we lose the awareness of our physical surroundings while we engage the spiritual realm.

I consider *translocation* to be the supernatural movement of our physical body to a different location by the power of God. (Ian Clayton often uses the term trans-relocation to describe the same experience.)

The next six chapters describe the different ways in which we can travel in the spirit. These chapters are based on the relationship our spirit has to our body when we travel—or at least the perception we have of that relationship.

Chapter seven is an overview of the practice commonly called *astral projection*. Since many people are under the impression that Christian spiritual travel is the same as astral projection, we're going to look at both practices and compare them. The information I'm providing on astral projection is for comparison purposes only. It is not my intent to teach you how to practice it.

The five chapters that follow describe the different ways in which Christians experience spiritual travel.

In chapter eight, we'll discuss spiritual travel that happens when we are asleep.

Chapter nine covers the experience I call translation by faith in-the-body. This is when we travel while we are awake, but there is no perception that it we have traveled outside of our body.

In chapter 10 we'll discuss what I call translation by faith out-of-body. This is when our spirit leaves our body and we are aware of that separation.

Chapter 11 covers translocation. This is when our spirit and body travel together to a different physical location.

Chapter 12 covers spiritual travel when we are in a trance.

CHAPTER SEVEN

Is It Astral Projection?

THE MOST COMMON QUESTION I'M asked about traveling in the spirit—and it is frequently stated in the form of an objection—is whether the spiritual travel Christians practice is astral projection. We can't rely on what the Bible says to answer this question. The scriptures make no mention of astral projection. We could rely on popular beliefs and religious traditions, but these views are often developed in ignorance of the actual practice of spiritual travel. Even among Christians who are experienced with spiritual travel, there is little understanding about astral projection except among the few who have practiced it.

In order for us to know if astral projection and Christian spiritual travel are the same thing, we must analyze both experiences and look at their similarities and differences. There really is no other way to answer this question honestly and objectively. In this chapter we'll look at four cases of astral projection as reported by experienced practitioners and make note of them. Then in the following chapters, we'll look at the various modes of Christian spiritual travel, make note of those experiences, and compare them.

I've never attempted astral projection, so the information I'll provide on this subject is second-hand. I've done my best to find reputable sources of information. I did a fair amount of research on astral projection before writing this book. For those who are interested, I would recommend doing your own homework if you still have questions after reading the next six chapters.

I would like to make one thing clear: It is not my intent to teach you how to practice astral projection. For reasons which will soon become clear, I do not advise anyone to practice it, so the information in this chapter will be only as much as is needed to understand its basic principles. My only goal is to describe as best I can the experience commonly known as astral projection so that we may compare it to the form of spiritual travel I refer to as *translation by faith*.

While doing my research, I found that a few books were highly recommended by those who are familiar with the subject. I selected the two books that had the most positive and the most helpful reviews. These two accounts are taken from the book *Adventures Beyond the Body* by William Buhlman:

Journal Entry, October 4, 1972

I silently repeat an affirmation, "Now I'm out-of-body," for ten to fifteen minutes as I grow increasingly sleepy. As much as possible, I intensify my affirmations as I drift off to sleep. Almost instantly I'm awakened by intense vibrations and an electrical-like buzzing throughout my body. I'm startled, and an intense wave of fear surges through me. I calm myself down by repeating, "I'm protected by the light." My initial fear slowly dissipates as I visualize myself surrounded by a globe of protective light. I think of floating and feel myself lift up and out of my physical body. I feel light as a feather and float slowly upward. As I float away from my body I realize that the vibrations and buzzing have diminished to a slight humming sensation. Feeling more secure, I open my eyes and find myself staring at the ceiling two feet in front of me. I'm surprised that I've floated that high and instinctively think about looking at my body on the bed. Instantly, I snap back to my physical body and feel a strange vibration as my physical sensations quickly return.

Journal Entry, November 2, 1972

I awaken to the sound and sensations of intense buzzing. It feels as if my body and mind are vibrating apart. At first I'm startled by the intensity of the vibrations, but slowly I calm myself and focus my full attention on the idea of floating away from my physical body. In seconds I float up and out of my body and hover several feet above it. I notice that the buzzing noise and vibrations immediately subside after complete separation... I feel a slight tugging sensation as I fly higher and higher over the city of Baltimore. The tugging sensation increases and I think of my body. Instantly, I snap back to my body. My physical body is numb and tingling as I open my eyes.[1]

These were some of Buhlman's first attempts and they are typical of what one experiences during astral projection. Now let's look at the experiences of another man. Robert Monroe was a pioneer in the field of out-of-body travel, beginning his research in the 1950s. During his lifetime, he worked with psychiatrists, psychologists, biochemists, and other specialists. He was the founder of the Monroe Institute, a non-profit organization specializing in research and training for out-of-body travel. The Monroe institute has been used by the U.S. Military to train its employees. Below are two excerpts from Monroe's book *Journeys Out of the Body:*

First Excerpt:

It was a Sunday afternoon... I lay down on the couch in the living room for a short nap while the house was quiet. I had just become prone, when a beam or ray seemed to come out of the sky to the north at about a 30° angle from the horizon. It was like being struck by a warm light. Only this was daylight and no beam was visible, if there truly was one.

I thought it was sunlight at first, although this was impossible on the north side of the house. The effect when the beam struck my entire body was to

---

1. Buhlman, William *Adventures Beyond the Body* HarperCollins 2009 Kindle edition

cause it to shake violently or "vibrate." I was utterly powerless to move. It was as if I were being held in a vise.

Shocked and frightened, I forced myself to move. It was like pushing against invisible bonds. As I slowly sat upright on the couch, the shaking and vibration slowly faded away and I was able to move freely.[2]

Second Excerpt:

Afternoon. The vibrations came quickly and easily, and were not at all uncomfortable. When they were strong, I tried to lift out of the physical with no result. Whatever thought or combination I tried, I remained confined right where I was. I then remembered the rotating trick, which operates just as if you are turning over in bed. I started to turn, and recognized that my physical was not "turning" with me. I moved slowly, and after a moment I was "face down," or in direct opposition to the placement of my physical body. The moment I reached this 180° position (out of phase, opposite polarity?), there was a hole. That's the only way to describe it. To my senses, it seemed to be a hole in a wall which was about two feet thick and stretched endlessly in all directions (in the vertical plane).[3]

Analysis

The first thing I'd like to note is that those who experience astral projection nearly always do it while sleeping. There may be a few exceptions, but the vast majority of those who practice astral projection must first get their physical body into a sleep state. The brain operates at different frequencies depending on what the body and mind are doing. These frequencies produce different waves on an EEG. Each frequency range is given a different name. For the purposes of our discussion there are two frequency ranges we need to consider:

- Theta wave – (four – seven Hz)
- Alpha wave – (eight – 15 Hz)

---

2. Monroe, Robert *Journeys Out of the Body* Harmony 2014 Kindle edition
3. Ibid.

The Alpha range (between eight and 15 Hz) is the brain's operating frequency when we're awake during normal activity. Theta (between four and seven Hz) is the first frequency range of sleep. The brain operates at around seven Hz during the first moments of light sleep and just before waking. It's also the frequency range of meditation and it's easiest to experience spiritual travel at this frequency.

A term often used by those who astral project is *body asleep, mind awake*. This describes the fact that you need to have your physical body in a sleep state while your mind is awake. Most people use meditation or some other technique to keep mentally awake while their body relaxes enough to travel.

The second thing to note from the testimonies above is a predictable set of experiences that happen when the non-physical (astral) body separates from the physical body and begins to travel. Most people who practice astral projection experience strong vibrations and hear loud noises as they separate from their physical body. They experience other sensations, but these two are the most commonly reported. In fact, those who teach astral projection say that the way in which you know it's time to leave your body is by sensing these vibrations. Some have suggested that the vibrations are not merely a side-effect of astral projection, but the primary condition which makes it possible. Once the vibrations occur, you're ready to leave your body and travel in the astral plane. Other sensations, such as waves of energy passing through their body, disorientation, numbness, and fear are often reported during separation and when traveling out-of-body, though experienced travelers learn to control them.

A third thing commonly reported by those who experience astral projection is the awareness that they are indeed separated from their physical body. For those who astral project, there is never a question of whether they are "in" or "out" of their body. After their non-physical (astral) body separates from their physical one, it's common to drift toward the ceiling of the room they're in. When they look around, they often see their physical body sleeping. Once they are separated from their body, they're free to move about. Novices tend to travel only in the immediate area, but experienced travelers go to different planes of existence. Typically, the experience ends when the individual is suddenly brought back into their physical body. Sometimes they feel a tugging sensation and are violently pulled back into their body, but not everyone experiences this. Some reenter their bodies at will, and some do it more gently. As they return to their body, many report feeling vibrations, tingling, and numbness for a few minutes.

The Silver Cord

On occasion, those who practice astral projection see what is known as *the silver cord*. The silver cord is a tether that serves to connect the physical and non-physical bodies. It has been described in a variety of ways. Some describe it as a long, smooth cable of light about an inch wide. Others have described it as having the appearance of a thin, fibrous strand similar to a spider's web. Some describe it as resembling a Christmas tree garland. Those who have seen it attached to the body report seeing it anchored to one of several locations: the forehead, the middle of the back, the chest, or the back of the head. The tugging sensation some people feel while traveling in their astral body seems to be from increased tension on the silver cord. Not everyone who travels by astral projection has an awareness of it, but it is a subject of much discussion (and much concern) among these travelers. It is generally believed that if your silver cord is ever cut while you're traveling out of body, you can never return to your body.

The silver cord is referred to (though only obscurely) in the twelfth chapter of Ecclesiastes:

> *Remember Him before the silver cord is broken*
> *and the golden bowl is crushed,*
> *the pitcher by the well is shattered*
> *and the wheel at the cistern is crushed;*
> *then the dust will return to the earth as it was,*
> *and the spirit will return to God who gave it.*
> ECC 12:6-7 NASB

The silver cord is frequently mentioned in the discussion of near-death experiences. During the process of death, the physical body separates from the non-physical one. As it moves farther away, the silver cord is stretched and eventually, it is severed. At this point, according to near death researchers (and Ecclesiastes) it becomes impossible for the non-physical body to be reunited with the physical one. This point in a person's transition into eternity may be accompanied by the appearance of a representative landmark, where the individual must make a decision. The boundary between this life and the next may appear as a line on the ground, a river, a wall, a fence, a field, or some other object. It is usually something the individual must cross over or choose not to. Once this barrier is crossed, the near-death experience becomes an irreversible death experience.

The silver cord is of interest to near-death researchers and it's of vital concern to those who practice astral projection. It is however, of almost no interest to Christians who travel in the spirit. I've had discussions with hundreds of believers who have traveled in the spirit. In all those discussions, not once has the silver cord ever come up. None of the Christians I've spoken with have ever seen or felt the silver cord.

I'm not able to say exactly why Christians who travel in the spirit don't encounter the silver cord, but it is a subject that is foreign to them. It would seem that perhaps the mechanism of attachment for believers who travel in the spirit is different from those who practice astral projection. I won't be dogmatic about this point. I'm certain there may be a few believers who have traveled in the spirit and have seen a silver cord. But it does appear that one is much more likely to encounter it while traveling by astral projection. Perhaps one day, we'll understand more about the mechanism of attachment for the believer, but today it remains something of a mystery.

Dreams

A KEY CHAPTER IN THE Bible that illustrates traveling in the spirit through dreams is found in Daniel chapter seven. It can also be used as an access point to these experiences. When I say "access point" I mean a place where one may enter into an experience. Many have found that when they meditate on a particular passage of scripture, they can use it to engage the spiritual world and by faith, enter into a similar experience. In Daniel chapter seven, the prophet had what he described as a dream and a series of visions. To the casual observer this may not appear to be a case of spiritual travel, but as we examine it closer, perhaps you will agree that it is:

> *In the first year of Belshazzar king of Babylon Daniel saw a dream and visions in his mind as he lay on his bed; then he wrote the dream down and related the following summary of it.*
> DAN 7:1 NASB

"I was looking in my vision by night, and behold, the four winds of heaven were stirring up the great sea. And four great beasts were coming up from the sea, different from one another."
DAN 7:2-3 NASB

When the vision began, Daniel realized he needed to pay close attention. He focused his attention and "kept looking" into the vision as he noted in the following three verses:

"The first was like a lion and had the wings of an eagle. I kept looking until its wings were plucked, and it was lifted up from the ground and made to stand on two feet like a man,"
DAN 7:4 NASB

"After this, I kept looking and behold, another one, like a leopard..."
DAN 7:6 NASB

"After this I kept looking in the night visions, and behold, a fourth beast..."
DAN 7:7 NASB

In the next verse, Daniel was contemplating the horns that he saw. As he thought about their meaning, the Lord showed him another horn:

"While I was contemplating the horns, behold, another horn..."
DAN 7:8 NASB

As we focus our attention on the revelation we are shown in a vision, God will give us more information to further our understanding. As Daniel pursued the revelation he saw in the first vision, he was given a new vision: the throne of God the Father. In this series of scenes, part of the revelation pertained to things happening on the earth while part pertained to things happening in heaven.

It's not unusual to see heavenly scenes in visions and dreams. But it's easy to dismiss them as being nothing more than "just a dream." It's been my experience (and the experience of others) that when we have such dreams and visions, many times we are actually *in* the place that we see in the dream or vision—at least spiritually. Although there is no indication that Daniel's physical body left his bedroom, it seems likely that his spirit was in the throne room of heaven as he observed the following scene:

> "I kept looking until thrones were set up, and the Ancient of Days took His seat; His vesture was like white snow and the hair of His head like pure wool. His throne was ablaze with flames, its wheels were a burning fire."
>
> DAN 7:9 NASB

As he continued to observe the scene, it became apparent that he was witnessing a proceeding in one of the courts of heaven:

> "A river of fire was flowing and coming out from before Him; thousands upon thousands were attending Him, and myriads upon myriads were standing before Him; **the court sat**, and the books were opened."
>
> DAN 7:10 NASB

Finally in verse 13, Daniel saw Jesus appear before the throne of the Father:

> "I kept looking in the night visions, and behold, with the clouds of heaven One like a Son of Man was coming, and He came up to the Ancient of Days and was presented before Him."
>
> DAN 7:13 NASB

This scene is reminiscent of the scenes described by the apostle John in the book of Revelation. No one would argue that John did not travel in his spirit into the heavens. Can we know for certain that Daniel did? I don't think so. But I believe his spirit may have been taken there to witness these scenes.

What is Spiritual Travel?

It can be difficult to understand how spiritual travel happens when we sleep. In order to get a better grasp of what *is* and what *is not* spiritual travel, it may be helpful to describe it in more detail.

We tend to perceive the things that are sensed by our physical body, our spirit, and our soul all from a single perspective. We also tend to identify these perspectives as originating from one physical location. To travel implies movement from one location to another. When we travel in the spirit, our spirit either travels to a different location or views things from a different perspective. When we perceive this shift of location or perspective, we call it spiritual travel.

As we think about travel and location, we generally think in terms of *physical* location. Since our physical body relates to the world in physical terms, it's the default set of ideas and values we use to describe visual perspectives and movement. And here is our first problem: our spirit doesn't have its origin in the physical world. It has its origin in the spiritual world, which assigns different values to things like time, location, and distance. Physical location is more or less irrelevant when describing the movements of a spiritual body.

Our understanding of spiritual travel must account for the fact that our spirit is not limited in the same way our physical body is, nor can it be *located* in the same way.

Our physical body is confined to a narrow set of physical parameters, and we use certain terms to describe them. The physical body occupies a set amount of space. It can be located by a set of coordinates on a map or by global positioning satellites. It has a certain mass. All of these things describe the limitations of our physical body. These limitations apply to things which have their origin in the physical world, but they are not useful when describing our spirit. Location, mass, volume, and all the other terms we use to describe the physical body do not apply well to the spiritual one. Things that originate in that world have a different set of limitations imposed upon them. And while these limitations may be similar to the ones of the physical world, they're different enough that applying them to that which is spiritual will inevitably create confusion.

Now let's take a look at how different dimensions and realms are perceived by the mind. The physical world has three spatial dimensions and a fourth dimension of time. A line is said to have only one dimension: length. An imaginary being that lived in a one-dimensional universe can only perceive things in that one dimension.

A square has two dimensions: length and width. An imaginary being that existed in that plane of existence perceives everything in those two dimensions. The being which existed in the one-dimensional universe would have no ability to perceive the dimension of width since that dimension lies outside of its own experience. It would perceive a two-dimensional square as a one-dimensional line, due to its limited perspective.

If we were to add to this discussion a cube, we now have an object with the three dimensions of length, width, and height. A being which had its existence in a two-dimensional universe would perceive the cube to be a square, because it has no ability to perceive the third dimension of height. In the same way, the one-dimensional being would still perceive the cube as a line, because that is the only dimension available in that plane of existence. In fact, a sphere, a cube, and a coffee cup would all be perceived as a one dimensional line, because that is the only dimension in that plane of existence.

The point here is simply that any being which exists in a certain plane is limited in its ability to perceive things which exist in a higher plane, or one that has more dimensions. The three-dimensional universe is higher in order than the two-dimensional one, which is higher than the one-dimensional universe. And that is how we must understand the spiritual universe and the physical one.

The spiritual universe is not just different; it is a realm of existence that is higher in every way than the physical one. Any being that attempts to perceive the spiritual universe from the point of view of the physical one cannot view it accurately. It can only be perceived correctly from the spiritual perspective.

Our spirit is loosely connected to our physical body. Although we perceive this connection to be one that imposes limitations on the spirit's ability to travel, this is actually not the case. Our spirit is free to explore the spiritual universe with few restrictions. The experiences it has are passed on to our soul, through the mind, via the imagination. They're usually perceived by the mind as visions or daydreams if they happen during the day. If they happen at night, they are experienced as the usual nighttime dreams most of us have.

As our spirit moves through the spiritual world, it sees different locations and encounters different beings. These experiences are interpreted by the mind as a kind of dreamy, visual scene being played out in our imagination. Often, we classify them as the product of an overactive imagination and dismiss them as being "not real." The mind has difficulty registering them as being real, because it is used to experiences which stimulate the physical body—not the spiritual one. But in fact, these are the very real experiences of our spirit. When these things happen, we usually describe them as dreams, but in fact, they are one way in which our spirit travels.

The spirit and mind seem to be more susceptible to travel right after going to sleep or immediately before waking up. The reason may be because the mind is less focused on the physical world and it's easier to focus on the things of the spiritual world. Most of my spiritual travels occur while I'm sleeping. Sometimes I know where I am, but many times I do not. I've done many things while traveling in my sleep, but most often, I find myself praying for someone to be healed.

My friend Mitzi Hanna shared the following experience of spiritual travel that she had while sleeping:

> I began listening to Bruce Allen when I happened to come upon his teachings titled *Translation by Faith*. It was November of 2013. He was talking about how God at times had translocated people for them to be used in service for Him. I had read about Enoch and how he walked with God and then was taken. I'd also read about Phillip in the New Testament when an Angel appeared to him and sent him to the eunuch of Ethiopia and how he was baptized and as they came up out of the water the Spirit of the Lord caught Phillip away so that the eunuch saw him no more. When I heard Mr. Allen say it can still happen today I stopped listening and went right into prayer. I asked our Father if He would please take me somewhere because, as His servant, I had a great desire to be used that way. And that I knew if He did it for one, He could do it for me.

> Nothing happened that night, nor for many nights afterwards. I pondered this in my heart and brought it up occasionally in prayer, but I was content to leave it in His hands. My prayer was answered in the spring of 2015, as I went to sleep and had this experience.

I was in the Middle East on top of a second story building, dressed in a burka. The building's architecture clued me in immediately as to where I was, as I looked out over the city. It was late at night, not yet early morning hours, and it was dark, but there were lights on the buildings that illuminated the street below.

I saw a large crowd of perhaps 200 women on the street between two buildings. They were dressed in dark burkas. I was standing on the roof of a building about two stories high. I had boxes around me that were already opened and full of Bibles. It felt as if I had been there many hours, not like I had just arrived.

I was grabbing handfuls of Bibles and tossing them down to the women. As each woman grabbed the Bible I tossed down, she would quickly stash it under her Burka and slip on down the street. I worked quickly but I was careful to reach as far down as possible to toss the Bible to make sure they would have the best chance to catch them.

I was the only woman tossing the Bibles but there were four other women dressed in burkas standing beside me. They handed me the Bibles as fast as I could throw them. I was very excited but there was also an element of fear in my heart that if we were caught, it would be very bad for the women.

Over and over, as the Bibles were placed in my hands I leaned over the wall to toss them to the women below me. Our eyes would meet through our burkas. I could see the mixture of excitement and fear in their eyes as they hid the Bible and shuffled away down the street. It was also as if each woman was deeply thankful for what I was doing.

The street was made of a type of cobblestone and everyone was very careful to be as quiet as possible. But the sound of shifting feet and shuffling filled my ears. These were absolutely the only sounds that were heard. Not one woman spoke a word, as they reached for their Bibles and passed one another on their way. There were no men.

I saw my box was about to be empty and asked a nearby woman to get me the next box. She stood very still and whispered, "That is all we have." She then turned and ran away as I watched her go down some stairs on the side of the building. I felt an urgency to throw the Bible in my hands and to be able to also get away. My last remembrance was of me leaning over with the last Bible in my hand and throwing it quickly to a woman below, reaching for it.

It was then that I hit my bed hard and awakened my husband with my arms outstretched thinking I was still throwing Bibles. I quickly pulled at my clothes because I wanted to see my burka, only to find I was in my night clothes. I immediately knew it was not just a dream, that I had gone somewhere for the Lord to serve His people. I can't explain exactly why I knew this difference.

Translation by faith while our body is asleep can be used to transport us anywhere in the world where people don't know Jesus. But it can be used for other purposes. One of them is intercession. My friend Gale Gibson shared the following experience which she had one night while she slept:

Soon after being baptized in Holy Spirit I began to have intense dreams where I would wake up, sitting upright in bed, speaking in tongues. (Speaking in tongues is a way in which the Spirit of God prays through us. When we pray or speak in tongues, we generally do not know what we are saying, but God does.) Often there were vivid visions that would continue after I woke up... almost like the dream continued into a vision.

One night I had a dream where I was praying for a Middle Eastern man who was under a powerful demonic attack and had no Christian support where he lived. In real life, I had never met or heard of this man, and I thought it was just a dream.

But then I woke up and I found that I was sitting upright in bed, praying very loudly in tongues (this happens a lot.) And the dream continued as a vision, although I was fully awake. In the vision, other people began to appear in the room with me, and they were also praying in tongues. These people were from every tribe, tongue and nation. They materialized out of thin air, but they were very much *real*. They were dressed in all kinds of cultural apparel, being Asians, Indians, Africans... every color, every language, every age. I had a supernatural understanding that God had awakened all of us to pray for this one Middle-Eastern Brother in Christ, who was in dire circumstances. I don't really know whether we were "transported" in the body, but I am confident that we all joined together in spirit for the sake of this one elderly Middle Eastern man.

Sometimes God allows us to be translated to help avert tragedy. My friend Katie Regan shared this testimony:

The following happened in 2012. A couple weeks beforehand, I secretly asked God to let me go around the globe in the spirit to help people. I didn't know what I was asking.

I dreamed that I was up on a hill looking down. I wasn't sure if it was a physical hill, or perhaps part of the spirit realm. There were many people around me. I don't know if they were humans or angels. They watched. I looked down and saw a man with a gun standing in the midst of a lot of children. He was shooting wildly in all directions.

Suddenly there was a little girl with dark hair crumpled onto the ground next to me. She was small, maybe third or fourth grade, and a little heavy. She had been shot, but she was still alive. She tried to stand up, but couldn't walk and she fell to the ground again. I caught her in my arms and tried to carry her to safety. We were still up high on the hill.

The gunman was still shooting people. I looked for a bush to hide the girl under, but because the gunman was still shooting, I covered the girl with my body and waited.

I woke up in the early morning. I decided to write the dream down later and ask God about it. I didn't think it was hugely significant.

Several hours later, I saw on the news about the gunmen in Newton, Connecticut killing upwards of 27 people including at least 20 children, at Sandy Hook Elementary School. Strangely, I didn't remember my dream. But I did begin to shake and weep. I immediately fell to the floor and began praying in tongues. In my mind, I was surprised that my body and spirit were reacting with such intensity. My prayer in tongues became almost involuntary and fiercely violent. Part lament, part bold declarations and commands, part tender, comforting song. I began singing a lullaby in the spirit. I felt strange, like I was someplace else. Words can't describe it.

After I began to feel relief in my spirit, I stopped and got up from the ground. Then suddenly it hit me all at once; I remembered "the dream" I'd had the night before.

I don't understand it all. But I believe that little dark-haired girl is a real person, who I fully expect I'll be meeting someday. I believe that our spirits are not bound by time and space, and that as I slept, my spirit went to the future, to help that dark-haired girl in some way. I believe that my prayers and singing, after the event happened, actually went back in time and manifested during the shooting.

I don't understand all of this. But I want to do more. I want to travel, in and by God's power, while my body sleeps, to other places of the world and universe, to other times, to help people, to encourage, to sing, to create, to build, to war, to paint... to do whatever my heavenly Father is doing.

It's easy to dismiss dreams as being meaningless thoughts from a weary soul or figments of an overactive imagination. But many of the experiences we have while sleeping are in fact, encounters in the spiritual world. The more we choose to believe our spirit is engaging the realm of eternity in these experiences, the more of them we'll have and the more significant they will become.

Exercise

I've found it helpful to literally give my spirit permission to travel in the spiritual realm while my body is asleep. On occasions when I've done this, my spirit has traveled into the heavens for various purposes. In the Sermon on the Mount, Jesus said, "Blessed are the pure in heart, for they shall see God." (Matt 5:8) This is a promise from Him that we can see God. This exercise is simple. Before going to sleep, give your spirit permission to travel into the heavens and if you want, give it permission (or direction) to meet with Jesus or God the Father. Here are two examples of what you might say:

"I give my spirit permission to travel into the heavens and meet with Jesus at the River of Life."

Alternately, you might say, "I give my spirit permission to meet with God the Father in His garden."

-- **Notes** --

CHAPTER NINE

Translation by Faith: In-the-Body

WHEN OUR SPIRIT TRAVELS TO a different location, but our body is unaffected, it is known as translation by faith. There are two different experiences in which this happens: in-the-body, and out-of-body. Let me illustrate the difference between them:

Imagine that you were to receive a message from a friend who lives in another country and they ask for prayer. Now imagine yourself sitting in a chair and as you're praying, you see an image of them in your mind and at the same time, you're aware that you're still sitting in the chair. Now imagine that this person contacted you and said they saw you in their home, praying for them. The fact that they saw you in their home would be confirmation that you actually traveled there in the spirit. This would be a case of spiritual travel in-the-body, because you never had a sense that you had left your body. Now imagine the same scenario only this time, you have the sensation of leaving your physical body as you see yourself travel to pray for this person. If this were to happen, it would be a case of spiritual travel out-of-body.

There may in fact be no functional difference between these two types of transport. I'm not certain we can do anything in one that we cannot do in the other. Both are examples of translation and both are activated by faith. The difference may only be one of perception. I've chosen to write separate chapters on them, not because I believe they are substantially different, but because we perceive them differently and therefore, we describe them differently.

When I became interested in spiritual travel, I was working for an ambulance service in Tacoma, Washington. One night a friend and I had a two-hour conversation about some spiritual warfare he had done that involved translation by faith. His experience provoked me to try a few experiments of my own. At this time, I'd been giving a lot of thought to the nature of visions. I was used to thinking of them in terms of "God bringing images to me." But now I had begun seeing them differently. I wondered if a vision might be something more like my spirit going where there was something happening, and witnessing it in that location, firsthand.

The following day while I was on duty, I was dispatched to do a transport coming out of Tacoma General Hospital. As we parked the ambulance, I felt the Holy Spirit suggest that I might try a spiritual travel experiment. I got out of the ambulance and went inside. We were picking up a patient on the third floor, but I also had a friend who happened to be in the Intensive Care Unit with liver problems. The ICU was on the second floor. As I stepped into the elevator, I focused my mind on my friend and in my mind, I immediately saw another reality. I could see myself passing through the door of the elevator and then through the floor below the ICU. I passed down the hallway and instinctively knew which room my friend was in. I passed through the door to his room and observed him sitting in bed, wearing a hospital gown. I saw his wife sitting in a chair next to him.

Exercising my will, I decided to leave the ICU. I passed back down the hallway in the opposite direction I had come. I went back through the floor and the elevator door and was now aware that I was still standing in the elevator. This entire experience may have taken about ten seconds. The elevator door opened and my partner and I got out and went to his room in the ICU. Everything was exactly as I saw it in the vision a minute earlier. The only difference was the expression on my friend's face. When I saw him in my mind, he was smiling, but when I saw him with my partner, he appeared to be sad.

How do we explain such a phenomenon?

Perhaps I made this entire thing up in my mind. It's possible that I could have guessed which room my friend was in, that he was sitting in his bed and that his wife was in the room with him. It's possible, but this is an unlikely explanation. The fact that everything looked the same when I saw it in my mind as when I saw it with my partner seemed rather to confirm that I was not just making this up in my mind. I had actually traveled there in my spirit.

This seemed to me at first to be a typical vision—something I had been experiencing for a few years. But after receiving confirmation that I had actually been there in my spirit, I had to reevaluate what I thought I knew about visions. Since then I've had many similar experiences and received confirmation that what I saw in my mind was in fact what actually took place.

I'll admit I had some concern about this experience. At the time, I didn't understand the purpose for it and I didn't know many people who were having experiences like this. I had followed fundamentalist Bible teachers who often warned us about being deceived. The last thing I wanted was to fall into deception. But I felt like this first experience was something the Holy Spirit wanted me to do, so I decided to try a second experiment.

The following Monday, I was at a hospital where we would stay for long periods of time in case the hospital needed us to do a transport. They provided a small room for us with a couple of recliners and a TV. When I was there, I spent a lot of time sitting in the recliner, seeking God. On this day, I turned the lights out. I decided to try "walking" in the spiritual dimension. I got comfortable in the recliner and closed my eyes. Almost immediately, I saw a place in my mind's eye that looked like a farmyard at night. I saw a barn, a gravel driveway, and a tree bank about 100 feet away. Although it was definitely night time in this scene, it was only early afternoon in Tacoma. I tried to "move" in the spirit by using my will to go forward, toward the bank of trees in the distance. I was able to "walk" toward the trees. I looked down and saw my feet walking on the gravel driveway. Interestingly, in this experience, I saw that my feet had on hiking boots and what appeared to be military style pants, but in reality, I was wearing navy blue uniform pants and black leather boots. Watching my feet walk was easy, but as I focused my eyes in front of me, my forward vision was very unsteady. It was almost as if I was seeing the scene through a handheld video camera. There was a great deal of "bouncing" in my field of view. It was difficult to make out details in the scene, but I could tell I was approaching the line of trees. At this point, I decided I had accomplished what I wanted, so I opened my eyes and turned on the lights.

I'd like to offer some observations on what I experienced when I traveled in the spirit compared to what is typically reported by those who use astral projection:

In both my experiences, I never had a sense that my spirit had "left" or "separated" from my body. When a Christian experiences translation by faith that is in the body, there is no sense of separation between the spirit and body. Although I was able to view things that appeared to be in a different location, I also had an awareness that my physical body was still in the elevator in the first experience and in the recliner in the second one. At no time was I able to see my physical body from a perspective outside of it.

In addition, I was able to perceive these two realities (or perspectives) together, without confusing them. It was something like playing a very realistic video game, where one can sense both the reality that they are sitting in a chair, playing a game, and engaged in another activity in a different location.

I felt no vibrations and heard no unusual noises during either of my experiences. In fact, it was difficult to hear any sound at all, except that I did hear my feet walking on the gravel road in the second experience. Many of my spiritual travel experiences are completely without sound.

I see different scenes, but many times, I hear nothing at all. (This is not to be taken as a rule, as many Christians *do* hear things when they travel.)

Some believers have expressed the opinion that when we travel in the spirit, it must be initiated and controlled by God. Both my experiences were initiated by me, and not God. Although I did sense a prompting from the Holy Spirit, I never felt like either experience was a sovereign event, controlled by Him. I could start or stop the experience whenever I wanted or choose not to have it at all.

I did not feel as if either experience was something that could happen "by chance." Many people who astral project spend time meditating or repeating affirmations to help them travel before going to sleep. But there is never any certainty they'll actually travel on any given night. They may prepare for weeks or months and not astral project at all. When they do, it seems to be an almost random occurrence. This is not the case with the type of spiritual travel my friends and I experience. Once your ability to perceive the spiritual realm is operating fairly well, and you have sufficient faith, you can freely travel at will.

The return to my body was effortless. There was no sense of energy going through my body. There was no sense of being pulled back into it. I had no awareness of a cord being attached to me. I heard no noises. I experienced no fear or apprehension while traveling. I felt no disorientation or tingling when I returned. For the Christian, translation by faith in the body tends to be an enjoyable experience.

Nearly everyone who travels by astral projection must first enter a sleep state. Christians have the ability to travel under the guidance and power of the Holy Spirit. For those who translate by faith, much of our travel is done while awake.

One similarity between translation by faith and astral projection is mental preparation. I did spend a few minutes seeking God's presence before I traveled in my second experience. In subsequent travels, I've found it helpful to sit quietly and meditate on God and His kingdom in order to engage the spiritual realm. Those who practice astral projection typically spend some time beforehand mentally preparing. Astral projection seems to be activated by the mind and the will when the individual is prepared properly. Those who do it successfully report that it's mostly an issue of getting your mind prepared and focusing on that which you desire to do.

Translation is done by faith. But you might be wondering what exactly is *faith?* Faith is having a confident expectation that God will do what He promised to do. Let me describe what faith looks like as it pertains to healing:

I'm most successful at healing when I simply know in my heart (without any doubt) that God is going to heal the person I'm praying for. I often find strangers in public wearing slings and immobilizers around their shoulders. When I do, I'll ask if they want to be healed. If it happens that they have a shoulder injury, I'll simply tell them that God is going to heal them if they allow me to pray. Now, you might think I'm offering them false hope, after all, how do I know with certainty they're going to be healed? I have an incredible amount of confidence (faith) that God will heal shoulder injuries because I've seen hundreds of them healed already. After you've seen 15 torn rotator cuffs and frozen shoulders healed in a row, it's rather easy to believe God will do it one more time. That's what faith is—it's confidence that God will do a particular thing.

In a similar manner, translation by faith is a matter of choosing to believe that God is going to assist you in traveling and expecting that you will go somewhere. I sometimes refer to it as traveling with the Holy Spirit, because it is guided (to some degree) and empowered by the Spirit of God.

In both my experiences, I felt prompted by the Lord to try traveling. That's how He *leads* us. He gives us a prompting at the right time and may suggest the purpose and destination. Since He suggested it, and I knew of a few biblical examples where it had been done, I believed that I could do it. I closed my eyes and expected that I was going to travel somewhere and I did. Although astral projection and translation by faith both require some mental preparation, the preparation process itself is completely different. (We'll explore the preparation process in more detail in the next chapter.)

Who is in Control?

It has been suggested that as long as God is in control of the spiritual travel experience, everything will work out fine and that we should never try to initiate an experience ourselves or control it. Many believe the difference between astral projection and Christian spiritual travel is that astral projection happens when an individual initiates the experience, but if God initiates the experience, it is not astral projection.

This line of reasoning comes from a view that God is a sovereign deity who is in control of everything. If taken too far, this view has the potential to make us little more than pawns—unwitting participants in a game of fate having no free will. Although most believers understand that we do have free will, when it comes to spiritual travel, some will switch their view of God and embrace this model. Suddenly, God must be in control of everything.

I once believed God was in control of everything. This view led me to think that He sovereignly healed whomever He wanted and that I had no say in the matter. I now understand that He's delegated authority to me to enforce His will on earth. I'm His ambassador. Thus—some people are healed because I choose to exercise my authority and free will and set them free by releasing His power. His power and our free will work together. We cannot abandon our view of God and abdicate our responsibility simply because the subject has changed to one which makes us uncomfortable.

One problem with believing God must be in control is that this is not how spiritual travel is portrayed in the scriptures. A good example is the passage where Elisha initiated spiritual travel to eavesdrop on his servant Gehazi. It may be that the prophet received a word of knowledge or a word of wisdom from the Lord. But the choice to follow Gehazi in the spirit was Elisha's. It was not controlled by the Lord. God is not interested in creating mindless puppets. He is interested in raising up mature spiritual sons who know their true identity, exercise their authority, and operate in power the way Jesus did.

Although these experiences can happen in a way that seems almost accidental, or under the control of God, they are quite easy to initiate on our own. It's my belief that when God initiates such an experience sovereignly, He wants us to learn how to initiate it ourselves. Translation by faith usually occurs under the complete control of the individual.

I suspect that we prefer to believe God must be in control of such things, because deep inside, we don't trust our ability to discern light from dark, life from death, and good from evil. We're afraid of being deceived, and we believe if we put the control in God's hands, we can't be fooled. Yet the writer of the book of Hebrews taught that it was *our* prerogative to come before the throne of God—not the other way around:

> *Let us therefore come boldly to the throne of grace, that we may obtain mercy and find grace to help in time of need.*
> HEB 4:16

Here the writer clearly puts the responsibility on us. If we want to enter the heavens and come before God's throne to obtain mercy, revelation, or anything else, we have an invitation to come there. But God is not going to force us to come before Him. The solution to our poor decision-making is not thinking God must be in control of everything. It's growing in spiritual maturity so we can learn to make wise decisions ourselves.

This testimony was shared by my friend Daniel Bryant Cook:

> The first time I ever experienced traveling in the spirit, I didn't know what I was doing. I simply didn't realize it was a thing we could do. Here is a little background about my life: During that time, I wasn't the most outwardly righteous person. Now that I look back at these encounters, I feel like I was being trained for things to come.
>
> I had gotten into one of the roughest situations I could have picked. I got into a relationship with someone after being asked to minister to them and be a good influence in their life. I sought to help set them free from a heroin addiction. The parents of this individual seemed to continually pull on me to be involved with this young lady and I had not learned yet how to say no. She had undergone a mighty deliverance and saw me as a savior. However, soon after her deliverance, the drugs got the best of her again.

She would call me and tell me demons were in her home, stabbing her feet, and ask me to pray for her. I prayed many times and when I did, I would experience being there in her home. I could see the evil spirits and I would engage them in order to remove them. It seemed like a constant battle and it was always intense. The demons tried to hide from me as I would walk through her house (in the spirit) to cast them out.

All of this seemed normal to me and I did not understand that as I rested at home in my bed, I was traveling there to her home (in the spirit). I thought my imagination was just overly involved or that I was seeing in a pretend type of way what was happening. It would be several years before I understood that this was actually a form of supernatural transportation.

My friend Fern Pope shared this testimony:

I have had the blessing of spirit traveling. I don't share much yet, except with my youth home group. Two years ago, I was in worship for about three hours in my bedroom. I was dancing when I suddenly realized I was in an octagon room. (How I knew it was octagon I don't know, but I did.) Then a door I couldn't see opened and Jesus stood there smiling. His eyes were amazing. He said, "Come, dance with me." I hesitated because I was in pajamas and said, "Look what I'm wearing." He laughed and said, "I don't care what you wear. Come as you are." As I walked through the door to dance, I was in this beautiful forest and Jesus said, "Go back and tell the church, in order to enter my Kingdom—in order to do this—you enter *as* you are, not *what* you are. You enter as a child—devoid of your own thoughts and opinions." He looked at me so tenderly. "Now go in your pajamas and tell them this." I will never forget the love on His face. I was then instantly back in my room. I felt I needed to share this story. I have had more experiences and I am a little shy about sharing them, but I was greatly moved in my spirit to share with you. God bless.

This testimony is from my friend Margie Moormann:

During the school year, I stay at my granddaughter's preschool. They've given me a room, so for four hours I'm by myself in the room. Many days are spent with Jesus and Holy Spirit. One day I had a quick conversation with Jesus. I said "Use me where you need me. I'm willing!" There was an almost immediate response on His part and I was suddenly in a third world country.

115

I would say it was somewhere in Africa, but only because the people were dark skinned and I was walking in a very poor area. There were a few stray dogs scavenging for food, and people with loose clothing (it was hot) walking on a dirt road. There were naked or scantly clothed children running near the road. It appeared to be a busy area of town. I was walking on the dirt road, noticing my surroundings, and saw a woman sitting on the side of the road. Everyone ignored her as if she didn't exist. She had on a long cotton skirt and a blouse or top of some sort. The skirt caught my eye because she was sitting in the dirt with one knee bent upwards and her skirt covered her legs. She had a pottery jug in front of her, between her legs. As I walked closer to her, she glanced up at me and then looked straight into my eyes. Instantly I had the realization that she was looking at Jesus, not me! She was seeing Jesus coming toward her! I walked up beside her and didn't say a word, but put my hand on her head. Immediately, I could see inside the jug that water was filling the jug from the bottom! I didn't see where the water was coming from, just that the empty jug was being filled. People started gathering around her, looking in the jug. Then I was suddenly back in my classroom at my granddaughter's preschool.

Occasionally we experience translation and the only evidence of it is a vague impression that we were somewhere else for a brief moment. There is usually no one who can verify that we actually traveled anywhere. Other times we will be translated and have no awareness of it at all. In these cases, we only realize later that we were translated when someone reports seeing us in a place and we were certain we were not there, at least physically. Sometimes this experience is referred to as bilocation, because it is apparent that we were in two places at once. It is however, nothing more than translation; there just happens to be a witness to the event.

Here is a testimony shared by my friend Brook Magar:

I grew up in Kansas and moved to Kathmandu, Nepal as a missionary after college. While there, I worked with a ministry among homeless men who were drug addicts. I normally stuck to one area of Kathmandu where I knew many of the addicts personally and had close relationship with them.

One day a friend and I stumbled across a section of town called Teku, that we were not familiar with. (Our ministry was located in a different part of the city.) There was an entire road lined with women selling heroin and hashish. At the end of this street, there was a big, open field with all kinds of young people laid out, high and using drugs. Syringes covered the ground. There were lots of sick people there who needed serious help. For a couple of girls with a ministry to addicts, finding this place was like hitting the ministry jackpot! We stuck around Teku and talked to a few guys for a few minutes and then left. We never went back there because we didn't have peace in our spirits about it. When dealing with hard drug users it's best to know your limits and to work further away from where the "big money" is, so to speak.

Over the next several months we had a strong move of God within our ministry. Many of the men we worked with got miraculously saved and delivered from drugs instantly, through simple prayer and praying in tongues. We opened up a drug treatment center in partnership with a local Nepali church.

About six months after my accidental visit to Teku, I was walking down the street and two young men walked up to me. They struck up a conversation with me in Nepali, and were calling me by my first name. I was a little confused because I had never seen these men before, and of course I was a foreigner, so it seemed strange that they would know I could speak Nepali.

When I asked them who they were they laughed out loud and acted like I was joking! They said, "Of course you know us, Brook! You come out to Teku all the time and tell us about Jesus. You've invited us to your church so many times, and have been telling us about your new treatment center but you've never showed us where it is! We haven't seen you in a couple of weeks so we were wondering what happened and why you stopped coming to visit us! How can you say you don't know us? You are too funny." They thought it was hilarious. I talked to them for a little while and then walked away trying to figure out what had just happened. Did they know someone else that looked like me? But they knew my name!

When I went back home and prayed about it, I was reminded of a prophetic word that my pastor had given me a few months prior, during a trip back home to the USA. I got out the cassette tape that they had recorded of the prophecy for me, and I was a bit shocked to remember that he had prayed that the Lord would translate me in the spirit to places where He needed to use me, and that my spirit man would be ministering to people in places where I wasn't physically present. I remember when I had originally heard that word I thought to myself, Wow, that would be cool, but I guess I'll never know if it happens. Well, now I had evidence.

Later, I started dating my boyfriend (now husband) who is Nepali and every time we would drive around to different parts of the city he would freak out because all kinds of rough looking people would pass us in the street and call out to me by name like we were close friends. He would always ask me how I knew every addict in the city. And I would just tell him, well I don't, but apparently they know me!

Although these experiences may not seem very dramatic when they are happening, in-body translation by faith can be used to accomplish some important things. It can help with healing and deliverance. It can be used to minister to people in other nations, and it can allow us to meet with Jesus in person. If you ask me, that's pretty cool.

Exercise

Translation by faith in-the-body is a relatively easy thing to do. It can be done anywhere at any time. Simply close your eyes and focus your mind on someone or something you'd like to visit. Perhaps you'd like to meet with Jesus or maybe visit someone in a hospital who needs prayer. The goal here is not to come up with an image in your imagination of what you think they may look like. The goal is simply to allow the Holy Spirit to take you there and show you the actual person or place. If you see a person, note whether they seem to be aware of your presence and if they are, you might interact with them. If at a later time you're able to confirm that they saw you, it might be good to record the details in a spiritual journal.

Notes

Notes

CHAPTER TEN

Translation by Faith: Out-of-Body

IN THIS CHAPTER WE'LL DISCUSS translation by faith where the spirit travels and the body is unaffected, but the traveler has the sensation of being out-of-body. To begin I'd like to share a fairly well-known case of translation by faith out of the body.

John G. Lake (1870-1935) was a man of vision with a goal to bring the fullness of God to every person. He lived as a missionary in South Africa in the early 1900s. During the years he lived there, he planted more than 100 churches. The following is Lake's account of an experience he had one Sunday while praying:

> At a Sunday morning service, before public prayer was offered, a member of the congregation arose and requested that those present join in prayer on behalf of his cousin in Wales (7,000 miles across the sea from Johannesburg), that she might be healed. He stated that the woman was violently insane

and an inmate of an asylum in Wales. I knelt on the platform to pray, and an unusual degree of the spirit of prayer came upon my soul, causing me to pray with fervor and power. The spirit of prayer fell upon the audience at the same time.

The people ordinarily sat in their seats and bowed their heads while prayer was being offered, but on this occasion 100 or more in different parts of the house knelt to pray with me. I was uttering the audible prayer; they were praying in silence.

A great consciousness of the presence of God took possession of me. My spirit rose in a great consciousness of spiritual dominion, and I felt for the moment as if I were anointed by the Spirit of God to cast out demons.

My inner, or spiritual, eyes opened. I could see in the spirit and observed that there was a shaft of seeming light, accompanied by moving power coming from many of those who were praying in the audience.

As the prayer continued, these shafts of light from those who were praying increased in number. Each of them reached my own soul, bringing an increasing impulse of spiritual power until I seemed well-nigh overcome by it.

While this was going on, I was uttering the words of prayer with great force and conscious spiritual power.

Suddenly, I seemed out of the body and, to my surprise, observed that I was rapidly passing over the city of Kimberley, 300 miles from Johannesburg. I was next conscious of the city of Cape Town on the seacoast, a thousand miles away. My next consciousness was of the island of St. Helena, where napoleon had been banished, then the Cape Verde lighthouse on the coast of Spain.

By this time it seemed as if I were passing through the atmosphere observing everything, but moving with great lightning like rapidity.

I remember the passage along the coast of France, across the Bay of Biscay, into the hills of Wales. I had never been in Wales. It was new country to me, and as I passed swiftly over its hills, I said to myself, these are like the hills of Wyoming along the North Dakota border.

Suddenly, a village appeared. It was nestled in a deep valley among the hills. Next I saw a public building that I recognized instinctively as the asylum.

On the door I observed an old fashioned 16th Century knocker. Its workmanship attracted my attention and this thought flashed through my spirit: That undoubtedly was made by one of the old smiths who manufactured armor.

I was inside the institution without waiting for the doors to open and present at the side of a cot, on which lay a woman. Her wrists and ankles were strapped to the sides of the cot. Another strap had been passed over her legs above the knees, and a second across her breasts. These were to hold her down. She was wagging her head and muttering incoherently.

I laid my hands upon her head and, with great intensity, commanded in the name of Jesus Christ, the Son of God, that the demon spirit possessing her be cast out, and that she be healed by the power of God. In a moment or two, I observed a change coming over her countenance. It softened and a look of intelligence appeared.

Then her eyes opened, and she smiled up in my face. I knew she was healed. I had no consciousness whatsoever of my return to South Africa. Instantly, I was aware that I was still kneeling in prayer, and I was conscious of all the surrounding environment of my church and the service.

Three weeks passed. Then my friend who had presented the prayer request for his cousin came to me with a letter from one of his relatives, stating that an unusual thing had occurred. Their cousin, who had been confined for seven years in the asylum in Wales, had suddenly become well. They had no explanation to offer. The doctors said it was one of those unaccountable things that sometimes occur. She was perfectly well and had returned home to her friends.

From the book *Adventures in God* by John G. Lake (this story is part of the public domain).

Lake's experience might seem extraordinary, but as we will soon see with the testimonies you're about to read, they are intended to be normal. I believe these experiences are available to anyone who wants to have them—and they're made available when we choose to believe. Lake simply chose to engage the spiritual realm and traveled thousands of miles to set a woman free of a demon.

Here's a testimony shared by my friend Lisa Perna:

I have had these sleep-dream experiences where I'm not quite fully awake, but I'm not very aware of my surroundings, either. I can feel my body and my bed and then I begin to feel the presence of the Holy Spirit. All of a sudden, I feel this electric current that quickly rushes through my body. I go in a comatose-like trance and there is no pain. Next, I can literally feel my spirit being pulled out of my body. For a few moments, I hover over my body. After that, then whoosh! My body feels like it's been vacuumed up. This has happened to me many times at night around 3:00 am. I never really remember much from these experiences, but I feel my spirit coming back into my body.

One afternoon the experience changed slightly. I was home with a cold. My husband suggested I take a nap… three times. I finally gave in and went to my room. I decided I would try to get some sleep. I'm not a nap person, so I put on the TV hoping this would help. Within the hour, I started to fall asleep. I could faintly hear the TV playing and I could feel the mattress under my body. All of a sudden, the sound of electricity pulsed through my body. I felt my spirit being pulled out again. I felt the whoosh like being sucked into a vacuum. The next thing I remember was standing in front of a huge sink. I had never seen anything like it before. It was the size of a feeding trough for animals. I could see five faucets protruding of out the walls. Inside, was a very thin metal bar, which somehow I knew held the soap.

There were two women there, one on either side of me. They seemed to be Middle Eastern because they had these veils wrapped around them. I didn't look at these women, but I knew they were there. I quickly surmised this was a public bath house of some sort. The next thing I saw was the water that filled the sink. It was milky colored. I then heard God say "Put your finger in the water." I then put my right index finger into the water. To my amazement the water separated from my finger. I could see clear water as the milky water pulled away. Then the Lord said, "Now, drink it!" I bent down to drink the water, but instead my whole head was submerged. I could hear the women screaming with excitement. I quickly pulled my head out. My wet hair flung back, leaving me completely drenched. I could feel the beads of water rolling off my nose and running down my face. Suddenly, whoosh! I was back in my bed. I'm still not sure why I went there or what it represented. The only thing I knew for sure is I couldn't have made that sink up. I searched online and sure enough, I found one just like it!

On the surface, Lisa's experience might seem similar to astral projection. She felt energy going through her body at the time her spirit separated from her body. She also clearly noticed that her physical body was lying on the bed and that she had left it. These are common features of astral projection. But let's take a closer look.

A feature one always expects to hear about when astral projection is involved is a sense of vibrations. But Lisa felt none. And although it's possible the electricity she felt was the kind associated with astral projection, it is equally possible that it was merely the power of God rushing through her body as is commonly reported by those who experience a sudden manifestation of His presence. During the experience, Lisa did not hear the noises one typically hears during astral projection. She did hear what she described as something like electricity passing through her body, but it was not the loud screeching sound typically reported during astral projection. Those who astral project generally find themselves, upon separation, in the room in which their physical body is located. They must then travel from that location. Lisa was immediately taken—and here, we must assume it was by the power of God—to another country on the other side of the globe. That is certainly not something one would expect if they were astral projecting. There are from time to time unusual experiences like Lisa's, but if we examine them closely, it isn't hard to distinguish between cases of translation by faith and astral projection.

My wife had an experience where she traveled out of her physical body. She had been asking God to show her things in the spiritual world for some time. One day, just after lying down to take a nap, she found that she couldn't sleep. Suddenly she became aware of the sound of a radio clearly playing in our bedroom. (We don't have a radio in our room.) So she got up out of bed to find out where the sound was coming from. As she did this she became aware that she was still lying in bed while also being conscious of the fact that she was standing in the middle of the room. She was literally in two places at once, or at least that's how she perceived things. Next, she saw a ridiculous-looking demon quickly running toward her from the hallway leading to our bedroom. The demon looked something like a crudely constructed gray fabric doll about 18 inches tall with sewn on eyes, nose, and mouth. She immediately sensed it was evil, but had no fear of it. The demon ran toward her and she knew she had to kill it. She grabbed it around the throat and strangled it. At this point, the part of her that was standing in the room came back into the bed. As her spirit and soul reunited with her body in the bed, she heard a whoosh sound and suddenly felt the full weight of her body in the bed again.

In this experience, she was literally translated into an event that was occurring in the spiritual world. She became a primary participant of something happening in the spiritual world while her participation in the physical world was temporarily put on hold. After the experience was over, her primary experience was again based in the physical world. The experience provided several benefits to her: It made her more aware of the realities of the spiritual world and just how closely it parallels the physical one. It also made her more aware of the presence of demons and it gave her a bit more determination to do battle against them.

The next question is: since we can travel out-of-body, is there a way to do it *intentionally*—and without using astral projection?

My friend Michael Van Vlymen has written two books on spiritual travel. *Translation By Faith: Moving Supernaturally for the Purposes of God* is a workbook he co-authored with Bruce Allen. *Supernatural Transportation: Moving Through Space, Time and Dimension for the Kingdom of Heaven* is a collection of testimonies and teaching on spiritual travel. Michael has graciously allowed me to share an excerpt from the second book, which addresses out-of-body translation by faith:

As I would go to my prayer chair at night after everyone in the house was asleep, I would focus on the Lord. I prayed and worshipped, meditated on the scriptures and just pictured being with Him. Sometimes I would get so relaxed, I would fall asleep. Many other times I would pray all night.

It was comfortable. I felt secure just worshipping God and pressing into Him. There were no distractions or worries, no fears or doubts, just me and the Lord in communion. As I would pray and worship in the comfort of my prayer chair, if I felt myself getting sleepy, sometimes I would get up and walk through the house while praying. It's a great way to continue in prayer and not fall asleep. I was finding that my soul or my body wanted to be satisfied even at the cost of missing a visitation from God. Being tired is a strong pull.

So I would get up and walk through the house and pray. Usually, I would take the same path and do laps through the house. Some nights this would go on for a long time. You have to understand—it wasn't just about logging hours for my journal. It was about praying until I connected with the heavenly, spiritual reality.

One evening as I was praying in my chair, I felt myself growing tired, so I got up and began going through the house, doing my nightly prayer covering. When I had gone through the whole house and made it back to my prayer chair, my body was still in the chair. I looked at my body sitting there in the chair and it threw me a bit. I had done my entire nightly prayer routine with the complete function and awareness of a tangible, physical person, even though I was in the spirit.

What I have come to understand is that our spiritual man or our spiritual body is a tangible reality. What Paul wrote "... whether in the body or out of the body I don't know..." is so very true. The spirit man is just as real as the physical, perhaps even more so.

Stepping into the Spirit

Once I learned that I could actually move into the spiritual realm like this, I began doing it on purpose. I would repeat what I had done in prayer, numerous times, recreating my time of prayer and waiting on God and looking for the manifestation of moving from the physical to the spiritual. I also began learning to use my imagination to quicken the process.

The realization that I needed to use my imagination came after listening to a teaching on the "sanctified imagination" by my friend Dr. Bruce Allen. Many of the exercises and steps of faith that I do have been things that he shared with me early on or things that the Holy Spirit highlighted to me after our conversations. The Lord uses us all to help others. Bear in mind that as God uses one person to help you, He will then use you to help someone else.

The sanctified imagination can move you into the things of the kingdom. The sanctified imagination is your spirit man getting involved. It is reality. So realizing this, I began to actually "see" myself leaving my prayer chair in the spirit and walking around the house. I would "do" this prayer walk, in my imagination, throughout the house over and over. I walked through my house so many times in the natural with my eyes and senses seeing, feeling, and smelling what it was like, it was fairly easy to reproduce this in my imagination.

I walked around as before and prayed. What happened was I began to experience actually going into the spirit for my prayer walks. I would go in the spirit and pray in the spirit. Then after I was done praying, I would go back and rejoin my physical body.

As with anything else we do, we need to practice to make it a part of our lives. We don't start out preaching to ten thousand people, but rather to one. As we learn, the Lord gives increase. I have found that in this particular thing, it is easier to lay hold of if we learn in a safe environment, like our own home.

The bigger picture here is learning to yield ourselves to God; to move and listen and speak by His Spirit, so that we grow into maturity. That is His intention for us. The only way that we can do the things we are called to do is by His Spirit.

Not long after this, I began lying down on the floor to pray. I would go up to my bedroom and lay down on the floor beside the bed and I would pray. Because the floor was hard, it made it easier to stay awake and pray, yet being in a reclined position allowed me to relax to a degree. Again, I began getting up in the middle of the night to do my prayer walks and many times, I would come back to the bedroom and see my body lying on the floor, beside the bed.

The Spiritual Atmosphere

Being in the spirit, even in your own home, can be a learning experience. I noticed that in the spirit, our house looked different than it does in the natural. There were some rooms, such as the rooms we pray in a lot, where the room seemed alive and bright. Other rooms that were normally not used much had a much bleaker look and feel to them.

When you are in the spirit, you can see what's going on in the spirit in your home. I have seen many strange and wonderful things floating around the house from time to time. Numbers, shapes, lights and various other things fill the spiritual dimension around us. Do I always know what everything means? No, of course not. This, like everything else is a learning process.

As I encounter these types of things I ask the Lord for greater revelation about them.

I recall that on one occasion I was in the spirit and I was doing my nightly prayer walk. It was about three or four in the morning and I came upstairs to see my daughter Angie lying in the hallway floor next to our dog. Angie was in the spirit and her body was asleep in bed. At the time, she had no awareness of what was going on. I told her she should go back to bed and lay down. She said, "I will Dad. I just want to lay here with Julia a little bit." Her spirit was having a normal interaction and discussion with my spirit. The next day I found out that she wasn't even aware this had happened. This is true for most people. Our spirits function in the spiritual realm with no conscious awareness of it.

I began to venture out into the yard and around the house. I did the exact same thing that I had done before, only I changed locations. I would walk around the outside of the house in my imagination and eventually the shift happened and I would be in the spirit. I did notice something powerful concerning the manifestation of this. If the thing I saw myself doing in my imagination was something more extreme, such as imagining myself flying instead of walking or imagining myself standing on the roof to pray, the shift into the spiritual dimension seemed to happen faster.

I love being in the spirit and being outside. I pray sometimes early in the morning and go into the spirit and take a walk outside to enjoy the morning in the spirit. I feel the coolness of the air, the dampness of the dew and the sounds of nature coming to life. My senses are all there, only heightened. I can be in the coolness of the morning and feel it and enjoy it, but I never feel too cold, regardless of the temperature.

Because I was (and still am) adjusting in many ways, I did what many others have done in trying to take some kind of physical proof of having been in the spirit and going somewhere. I was looking for the inferior to give credibility to the superior. It just shows how strong those earthy, carnal perceptions can be.

Moving Physical Things with Spiritual Hands

I was in the spirit one morning walking around in the backyard and patio area, when I had a brilliant idea. I decided to take some of the mulch chips from the flower bed and place them on the air conditioning unit and then come back outside in the morning with my physical body and see the mulch there. This would corroborate my adventure in the spirit that morning.

So that is exactly what I did. I grabbed a handful of mulch and placed it on the air conditioner. The problem was that when I came back outside in the morning, it looked like about only half the amount of mulch that I had actually placed there. That only left me with more questions. I believe the Lord wants us to realize that the spiritual realm is the superior one and that we should think, and believe from that place, instead of constantly trying to prove the spiritual realm by what can be observed in the physical one.

Michael's testimony is extremely instructive. He seems to have experiences similar to those who astral project, but without experiencing the same sensations. He hears no noises, feels no vibrations, and is not brought back into his body suddenly. And there is another important difference worth noting. I've read many testimonies of astral projection. No one I know of has been able to effect a change on an object in the physical world while astral projecting. This is no small thing.

Those who study metaphysics have theorized that humans have many different bodies, one of which, is the astral body. Although I do not necessarily agree with these theories, I cannot disprove them. It's possible their models are valid and for the sake of this discussion, I will assume they are. It has been theorized that the difference between the physical and astral bodies is one of frequency of vibration. The astral body and astral plane are believed to vibrate at a frequency much higher than the physical plane and physical body. If this is indeed so, it would explain why it is difficult, if not impossible, to effect any change in the physical plane when traveling in the astral body. Bodies that exist in two different planes cannot affect one another, as we saw in the illustration of the one, two, and three-dimensional universes.

William Buhlman noted in his book the many times he tried to move things in the physical plane while traveling in his astral body. He set pencils on their erasers and tried to move them while traveling out-of-body without success. He attempted to blow out lit candles without success. According to metaphysical literature, physical matter vibrates at a frequency so low that it cannot be acted upon by an astral body, which vibrates at a higher frequency. The astral body vibrates at a frequency so high it's like a sound wave that passes right through solid objects. This is why a person traveling in their astral body can walk through solid objects such as walls and doors.

In contrast, Michael, when he traveled in his spiritual body, was able to pick up a handful of mulch. If he were traveling in his astral body, this should have been impossible. Yet he was able to walk through solid objects at will and was also able to pick up solid matter.

This is one reason why I believe translation by faith and astral projection are not the same thing. When a person travels in their astral body, they can only affect the non-physical plane. But when one translates by faith they can influence both the physical and the non-physical worlds. The other reason why I believe they are different is the sensation of vibration that is nearly universal to astral projection, but is almost unheard of when translating by faith. I'd like to offer a theory as to why this is so.

As you read about astral projection, it becomes clear that there is a transition that the mind goes through during this process. The transition is one of perceiving first the physical plane, which vibrates at a low frequency, and then the astral plane, which vibrates at a high frequency. As the mind adjusts to the change in vibration—to the change in frequency—what would one expect it to perceive during this transition?

Vibration.

As the mind first perceives the higher vibration of the astral plane, it senses the increased vibration. But as it adjusts to the new plane's vibrational frequency, the sense of vibration dissipates. That is, until the traveler returns to their body. At this point the vibrations are felt once more.

A person who is born again by the Spirit of God, on the other hand, is able to travel in the spiritual world in a way that does not involve astral projection. We do not travel in the astral plane, but a different one—the spiritual kingdom of God. Jesus said to Nicodemus that no one can enter nor see the kingdom of God unless he is born again (see Jn 3:3, 5). It is only after we are born of the Spirit that we can travel in this plane of existence. And I believe this is why our experiences, while being similar, have significant differences.

To make comparison easier, below is a list of features typically experienced by those who astral project and those who translate by faith.

Astral projection has the following features:
- Travel is nearly always done while asleep.
- The traveler nearly always experiences vibrations.
- The traveler may experience loud noises, tingling, numbness, fear, disorientation, and other uncomfortable sensations while traveling out of body and immediately afterward.
- The traveler is always aware of being out of body.
- The traveler may suddenly or violently return to their body.
- The traveler may be aware of the presence of a silver cord.
- The traveler may or may not successfully astral project after preparation.

Translation by faith has the following features:
- Travel may be done while asleep or awake.
- The traveler does not experience vibrations.
- The traveler may hear sounds and feel energy going through their body, but these sensations are not uncomfortable.
- The traveler may or may not be aware of being out of body.
- The traveler is not returned to their body suddenly or violently.
- The traveler is usually not aware of a silver cord.
- Once the traveler's faith is operational, they can travel at will.

Exercise

Michael Van Vlymen's method of traveling in the spirit out-of-body is to use his sanctified imagination to visualize himself walking around in the spiritual realm that surrounds him. Begin this exercise by getting in a comfortable position and setting your mind on God. The goal here is to "see" yourself leaving your chair (or wherever you are) and walking around the house or building you are in. You are going to use your imagination to visualize yourself walking right out of your body and engaging the spiritual realm. Do this exercise in your mind repeatedly. Try not to become discouraged if you don't have results instantly. It may take some regular practice before you begin to have success. As you practice, you will find your spirit at some point being able to move beyond your physical body. You may want to record what happens in a journal.

Notes

Notes

CHAPTER ELEVEN

Translocation

I CONSIDER TRANSLOCATION TO BE the supernatural movement of our physical body and spirit in unison to a different location by the power of God. (For those who are familiar with the teaching of Ian Clayton, he often uses the term trans-relocation to describe the same experience.)

The first time God spoke to me about traveling in the spirit was through a couple of dreams in March of 2010. In the first dream, I was translocated to Boston. My physical body materialized on a freeway off-ramp somewhere in the city and I walked to the nearest intersection. I asked a stranger for directions to Fenway Park. One man told me to get back on the freeway. A second told me to take surface streets and to be sure to get a hot dog at the game.

In a second dream, two close friends and I were being translocated as a group. We made three trips to different locations in all. Between the trips, we had time to discuss the experiences we had and the limitations we were given. I don't recall the specific limitations my friends were given, but before one of our trips, I was told not to eat anything until I returned.

In a different dream, I materialized on a freeway overpass. There was very little traffic on the freeway below. I was standing near a four lane ramp that was under construction. The ramp came from the freeway. Two of the lanes were for the off-ramp and two were for the on-ramp. Only half the ramp had been completed, so both the traffic coming off and the traffic going onto the freeway were using the off-ramp, which had a temporary lane divider set up. Now, I'd like to interpret the dreams.

It's obvious that the subject of the dreams is spiritual travel, and in particular—translocation. If the second dream is taken literally (and I do have an unusual number of literal dreams) it illustrates the fact that we can be translocated as a group. But if taken symbolically, the idea is that we might learn about spiritual travel as a group. It's possible both interpretations are valid.

The second thing to note is that there may be instructions we need to follow if we want to have these experiences. In the second dream, I was told not to eat anything until I returned. In the first dream someone told me to be sure to eat a hot dog. This suggests that following any instructions that we receive is important and we may need to watch out for those who would try to get us to disobey or forget about them.

The third thing to note is that one of my translocation experiences was simply for the purpose of going to a baseball park to watch a game. No healing. No intercession. No saving dying refugees. No handing out Bibles. Those things are wonderful and I'm glad God uses translocation for those purposes, but this time, it was just me and my heavenly Father going to watch a game. Would God allow us to have these experiences just for pleasure? I think He would. He's a wonderful Father.

The last thing from the dream I'd like to discuss is the freeway overpass scene. Although the rest of the scenes may be interpreted literally, this scene is definitely intended to be symbolic. In this dream, I believe freeways and cars represent a mode of transportation—a way in which we travel. And since the first dream revealed that the subject matter is translocation, the second dream seems to further reveal the Father's heart on that matter.

If we understand the entire scene as being symbolic of the present state of spiritual travel, we gain an understanding of a few things. First, as I stood on the overpass and surveyed the traffic below, there were very few cars on the freeway. This illustrates the idea that there are few believers right now traveling in the spirit.

Next, there is the matter of the off and on ramps. At the present time, there are only two lanes available for traffic to enter and exit the freeway—one lane in each direction. But there are two more lanes under construction, which when completed, will double the capacity for traffic. I would take this as confirmation that the Lord desires more of us to travel in the spirit at the present time, and that He is making plans to allow even more of His people to travel in the future.

Michelle Myers was kind enough to share this testimony of what seems to be a clear case of group translocation:

> I was driving a van with seven children in it. We were on a busy road, when we all suddenly realized we were "taken" to another road. It surprised us all, because everyone immediately felt and was aware that we were instantly moved over a mile away onto a different road with less traffic.
>
> I knew we had avoided danger, but imagine how pleasantly surprised I was, when even the youngest child said, "Mommy, angels moved the van or something."
>
> We all started worshipping, thanking the Lord. The children were around ages 14 down to six.
>
> Details: We were in Oklahoma City, driving on MacArthur Boulevard by Victory Church, when suddenly we were on Rockwell Ave, by a little airport strip called Wiley post.

It's impossible to say with certainty why the van was moved to a road a mile away, but the most likely reason was to avoid a collision or some other unseen danger. Just as the disciples were transported supernaturally in a boat, this family was kept from harm by being translocated in their van.

I've heard many testimonies of translocation over the years. For reasons I don't yet understand, they often involve people driving long distances. Many times the person who is translocated is in dire straits and only supernatural intervention by God will prevent a disastrous outcome. That's the case with our next testimony which happened to my friend Bryan Parks, who granted permission to share one of his experiences:

> I've had two experiences of supernatural transportation that happened soon after I entered the kingdom. Both involved me and my mode of transportation. The first involved me and my motorcycle. The second involved me and my car. Here's what happened during the first experience:

> I was on a trip on my motorcycle, traveling back to Indiana after having gone out to Portland, Oregon in 1980, the year Mt. St. Helens erupted. I had gone to Oregon with a neighbor with a promise of getting a job in the ship yards as a welder. The job never panned out. Actually, the whole story was a lie to get the guy a ride back home. The shipyards had been closed for some time and there weren't any jobs. So I head back disillusioned, both about people, and my own life. I got on my motorcycle and headed back to Indiana. By the time I got to Nebraska, I got in touch with a family friend, who let me stay overnight. The next morning, I continued my trek. The problem was—I was broke. I knew there was no way I would be able to complete the trip on the gas I had left in my tank. I drove as far as I could, hit the reserve switch and started praying.

> I felt compelled to reach into one of my empty pockets and pulled out a 20 dollar bill that wasn't there the previous night. I tried to convince myself that my friend had snuck into my pocket when I wasn't looking. I found a gas station and filled up the tank then continued the drive, knowing full well there was still no way I could finish the drive home. I began praying things like, "If this was You, Lord, I need more money to appear in my pocket." I began to remember times of supernatural transportation that were recorded in the Bible, and began to recount them before the Lord, saying, "If you could do it for them you can do it for me." By then, I was extremely low on gas and much in need of a miracle—however He wanted to do it.

Suddenly, I came to an area on the highway (on a clear day) that was covered in fog. I reduced my speed as I entered it and struggled to find the lines on the road. I can't tell you how long I was in the fog bank because it was as if I'd suddenly lost my sense of time. I also remember thinking it was like no fog I'd ever been in. There was no moisture at all, like there would normally be in a fog bank. I remember being very frustrated because I couldn't see, which is never a comfortable feeling when you're on a motorcycle.

I finally emerged from the fog into the clear, sunny day that it had been before, only to find myself about 30 miles from home. I started choking up as I realized that somehow God transported me and my motorcycle completely through the states of Iowa and Illinois. I now had plenty of gas left to finish the trip!

Like many people who have experienced supernatural transportation, Bryan focused on testimonies of others who had experienced the thing he needed. By focusing on the testimony of what God had done before, his faith that God would do it again allowed him to be translocated hundreds of miles.

Ian Clayton is considered by many to be one of the Christian pioneers of spiritual travel. He has graciously shared many of his experiences with audiences around the world. He had always desired some kind of physical evidence that he had translocated to a different part of the world, but always came back empty-handed. During one experience, when he was about to return from talking with an Indian shaman about God, he reached down to pick up a handful of sand to take it with him as evidence of his travel experience. The Lord told him, "If you take that back, you'll never go again."

He dropped the sand and returned home. For the next four years he never had any evidence of the fact that he had physically translocated to distant lands. One day, he traveled to an eastern country. He was in a house with a woman and three children and bullets were coming into the house. The woman asked who had sent him. He replied that God sent him. He could tell she was a Christian by the way she responded. To get the woman and her children to safety, he lifted them over a wall. While he was climbing over the wall, his hands slipped and he struck the area below his rib cage on the wall. He fell from the wall to the ground and when he did, he awoke in his bedroom. In the morning, he could see bruises from where he had hit the wall. He finally had the evidence he wanted.

One thing to note is the fact that Ian did not speak the language this woman spoke nor did she understand English. As Ian related the story, in his mind, he heard himself speaking English. When she responded, she was not speaking English, but he still understood her. Many people who travel in the spirit to foreign lands have reported speaking to people who did not know their language, and yet it never hindered their conversation.

I won't be dogmatic about this, but it's my belief that the physical translocation of our bodies is a two-step process. The first step is that we must develop our ability to ascend into the heavens (perhaps a better description is to enter the kingdom of heaven) as a spirit being, while leaving our physical body here on the earth. Ascending into the heavens is something we use our own free will to do. I believe the second part comes later; after we've learned to ascend into the heavens. Once we've mastered the first part, God may release to us the ability to have our physical bodies ascend into the heavens along with our spirit, then come back into the earth in a different location. (That is why I believe we must first master the ability to ascend into the heavens.)

If you are a born again believer, you can ascend into the heavens any time you like, as often as you like. The trick is renewing your mind to the truth that you are a spirit, living temporarily in a physical body. My understanding at this point in time is that the physical translocation of your body is at the complete discretion of God. He decides when you leave, where you will go, and what you will do once you get there. This experience requires complete obedience. The revelation I have and the testimonies I've heard make it pretty clear that disobedience will end your translocation experiences.

Once you begin translocating physically, God may have an assignment for you. If the assignment takes you to a foreign nation, language won't be a barrier. If it requires resources you don't have, He'll provide whatever you need. It will often involve prayer, healing, or some other activity. God can use physical translocation for a multitude of purposes.

It can be used to save us from tragedy. It can be used to assist us in ministering to people in distant lands, in places where safety might be a concern and at times when we would not normally be able to do the things we must do.

Exercise

Translocation seems to be done at the discretion of God, though I don't want to remove the possibility that one day, when we've sufficiently matured into His sons, we will learn to do it at our own discretion. The people who are having these experiences seem to have completely surrendered their time to God. I would recommend as an exercise giving your time to God, unconditionally. Make a habit of asking Him to use you in any way He sees fit at any time, even if it might be inconvenient for you. If you remove the restrictions on your time and talents, it gives Him more freedom to take you places to do His work.

Notes

— **Notes** —

Notes

CHAPTER TWELVE

Trances

ONE OF THE RAREST AND most mysterious forms of spiritual travel is what the Bible refers to as a trance. A trance is a state of being where we have little awareness of what is happening in the physical world because our soul and spirit are fully engaged in the spiritual one. The following is an account taken from the book of Acts where the Apostle Peter was given revelation from God in a trance:

> *The next day, as they went on their journey and drew near the city, Peter went up on the housetop to pray, about the sixth hour. Then he became very hungry and wanted to eat; but while they made ready, he fell into a trance and saw heaven opened and an object like a great sheet bound at the four corners, descending to him and let down to the earth. In it were all kinds of four-footed animals of the earth, wild beasts, creeping things, and birds of the air. And a voice came to him, "Rise, Peter; kill and eat."*

But Peter said, "Not so, Lord! For I have never eaten anything common or unclean."

And a voice spoke to him again the second time, "What God has cleansed you must not call common." This was done three times. And the object was taken up into heaven again.
ACTS 10:9-16

While he was in the trance, Peter was given understanding of God's plan for the gospel. The revelation was not given to him plainly, but symbolically. And because it was given symbolically, he did not understand it. The meaning was about to become clear as the people it pertained to were on their way to meet him while he was in the trance. The explanation was then given to him by the Holy Spirit:

While Peter thought about the vision, the Spirit said to him, "Behold, three men are seeking you. Arise therefore, go down and go with them, doubting nothing; for I have sent them."

Then Peter went down to the men who had been sent to him from Cornelius, and said, "Yes, I am he whom you seek. For what reason have you come?"

And they said, "Cornelius the centurion, a just man, one who fears God and has a good reputation among all the nation of the Jews, was divinely instructed by a holy angel to summon you to his house, and to hear words from you." Then he invited them in and lodged them.
ACTS 10:19-23

The "unclean" animals he saw in vision while he was in the trance were symbolic of the Gentiles, whom the Jews thought were "unclean" or not good enough to be accepted by God. Peter needed to have his understanding corrected. Once that happened, he became the first disciple to preach the gospel to the Gentiles.

I'm fortunate to know a man named Tom Calkins, who experienced a trance for five hours one night. His testimony is an excerpt from the book *Adventures in The Glory*, which Tom co-wrote with his wife Pat.

Tom and Pat would call themselves ordinary believers, pursuing an extraordinary God. This is the retelling of an experience that happened in church a few years ago. It was first told publicly at a class held in Lacey, Washington during a session of their church's school of supernatural ministry. I was in the class as a guest when Pat and Tom shared the experience and showed a number of videos that were recorded while it was happening. The events are told from two perspectives. First, we'll hear Pat's description of what she saw. Then Tom will explain what he experienced. Their testimony is being republished with their permission.

Tom's Introduction

Our church, Revival Town, generally holds three conferences a year. They are always a highlight because people from our whole region come, expecting to receive a great deal from God, to experience a concentrated degree of His Glory, and to be flooded by His Presence. God never disappoints!

At one of these conferences, I had a very unusual experience. It was in the evening service of the first day of a three day conference. We had recently undergone some personal transformation. Since then, Pat and I have enjoyed helping in any capacity that we can. We can't help musically. We know our limitations, and that is definitely one of them. However, we are pretty good with the busy work. Pat and I assist with set up before the meetings begin and then greet people at the doors as they arrive. Then as the meeting proceeds, we assist with ushering and ministry needs, and after the meeting we help with clean up and eventually lock up and secure the building after everyone has left.

To be honest, being so busy with duties during a meeting tends to distract from the spiritual side of the meeting. But we learned early in our Christian lives that you can't out-give God. He will always more than repay our giving. Which brings us back to the meeting... the service was nearly finished and we were heading into a time of closing worship and personal ministry time. I noticed that Pat had already gone forward, as had dozens of others, and I could tell there was a heavy Presence of the Lord settling on the altar area of the church. I decided to leave my post at the back of the church and go forward. As I entered the area I joined with the crowd and stood next to Pat, lifting my hands in praise to the Lord.

I had barely begun to worship, when I felt a strange sensation on my arms. I was wearing a short sleeved shirt and I could feel an intense heat on my forearms. It was as if someone had turned on a heater right in front of me. I turned and asked Pat, "Can you feel that?" Then I turned back to worshiping without waiting for her response. At that very moment, I began to experience the most unusual thing that has ever happened to me...

Pat's Side of the Story

There was a large group of us who had gone forward for a little post-service worship following the end of the regular service. Tom came up and stood right beside me. The music was playing softly and there was a very sweet Presence of the Lord there. I was standing on one side of Tom and our friend Diane Rieger was on the other, to his right. The worship leader was singing, "come up here."

At first, I didn't realize that anything unusual was happening because Tom was just standing there with his hands raised in praise. Except, there was one thing that did catch my attention. At one point, Diane began to shake and she looked like she was going to fall over and sure enough, she did! She grabbed onto Tom's arm and, swoosh, down she went. The part that was extremely unusual was that Tom made no attempt whatsoever to catch her. He just stood there, not moving and not reacting to the fact that she had just fallen, not even seeming to notice.

That struck me as odd, because Tom is always right there with the other catchers, "catching" as people fall over when the power of God touches them. It is one of the things he enjoys most, because he is closest to the action, the spiritual action, where the Spirit of God is moving strongly. But this time, someone fell right beside him, even grasping onto his arm, and he just stood there.

But Diane was fine, I checked. It seems that God Himself had caught her, or had an angel do it. Either way, she landed as softly as a feather. I quickly dismissed the incident, not giving it a second thought. It wasn't until much later that I began to notice that things were not "as usual" with Tom. Long after I had returned to my seat, I noticed that his position had not changed, not even slightly. He was still standing motionless, with his eyes closed and hands slightly raised. The music was winding down. The meeting was drawing to a close and people were beginning to leave. The cleanup crew was starting to spiff up the place. One hour had passed. At this point, I had the presence of mind to grab my camera and start taking pictures.

By now, a curious few had started to gather around Tom, who remained motionless. He looked like a mannequin in a store, frozen in place, just standing there with his hands positioned in praise. I had been careful not to do anything that would distract him, such as talk to him or touch him, because I did not want to interfere with anything that the Lord was doing. But it was becoming more and more obvious that something very strange was taking place. As time passed, more and more people were gathering around.

They were all talking and wondering what the Lord was doing with him. Eventually, someone touched his hand. No response. They began talking to him. No response. Some even began posing for pictures with him, and still... no response.

We were all having a great time laughing and speculating about what was happening. The whole while, Tom just stood there motionless. Two hours passed. Then two and a half, then three. By then, just a few people remained in the building. The question was now changing from, "What is going on with Tom?" to, "What do we do with him?"

There did not seem to be a sense of panic. No one was asking, "What is wrong with him?" They were just wondering how to handle the situation. After all, we needed to lock up the building and that was usually Tom's job, but clearly, he was in no condition to do it. Fortunately, the key to the building was on a lanyard around his neck. Someone removed it so they could do the locking up. But still the question remained, "What do we do with him?" Do we all just go home and leave him standing there?

No, that was not an option. Everyone else could if they wanted to, but not me. And not my friend Mary either. She was in this thing for the long haul, if that is what it took. We had been calling Jason Phillips (the pastor) every few minutes to keep him posted. He had left just before all this began in order to get the visiting guest speakers to his house so they could get a good night's rest for tomorrow. Finally, the topic of transporting Tom came up. I don't remember whose idea it was, but I liked it better than leaving him standing. We would take him to Jason's house, since he and the other guys there could help carry him in. However, our car, a VW Bug, was completely inadequate for carrying a "six-foot board." So, the decision was made to put him in the back of Mary's roomy Honda Pilot. I would follow in our Bug.

Two of our friends, Eddie and Eric, tipped Tom over backward, grabbed onto either end of him and carried him to the waiting car. He was so stiff that he didn't even bend in the middle. As they approached the car, Eric tripped over a big rock and nearly dropped his end of Tom, but Tom didn't flinch. They positioned him into the back of the car and scooted him in the rest of the way by pushing on his feet. Now he was flat on his back, with his hands still up as they had been while he was standing.

Honestly, it didn't look good. He looked… well, you can guess. And for the first time, I was beginning to worry. No one who was there had ever witnessed anything like this before. Even still, everyone seemed quite confident that he was okay. One friend even said, "I wish it was me." Nevertheless, I couldn't help but wonder if he was going to be like this forever? My fears, for the time, I kept to myself.

Before we took off for Jason's house, Mary informed me that she needed fuel so she would have to stop at a gas station. "No! Absolutely not!" I said. "You'll just have to take your chances. You are not stopping for gas with a frozen body in the back seat of your car! Someone will call the police!" She agreed and decided to just hope she had enough gas to get to Jason's. Fortunately, she did and when we arrived, Jason and the ministry team came out to the car. They couldn't believe what they were seeing. There lay Tom, flat on his back with his hands in the air, arms bent at the elbow. Jason climbed into the back of the car to survey the situation. After checking it out, he turned and looked at Mary, the ministry team, and me, and declared, "I think it's the Lord." Which to me, meant he was as clueless as the rest of us. I had hoped he would say something like, "Oh, nothing to worry about. I see this all the time. No big deal."

Although his statement did little to alleviate my fears, the way he said it came across in such a humorous manner that we all laughed. Once the laughter subsided, it was time to try to get Tom into Jason's house. As Jason and a couple of the other guys pulled on his feet, out he slid, still as stiff as a board. Jason took his feet and Mary took his right shoulder and one of the guest speakers took his left shoulder. They lifted him up and started the long trek across the yard toward the house.

And where was I during all this? Following behind with my camera, snapping pictures, vacillating between laughing at the spectacle, and fighting the nagging fear that something was terribly wrong with Tom. We were all quite grateful that it was dark outside because the scene surely would or could have caught the attention of a neighbor or two. The only light on the event was the occasional sudden, brief, flash of my camera.

About half way across the lawn, the man at Tom's left shoulder lost his grip and completely dropped his side of Tom. Fortunately, he was able to catch him by the elbow on his way down and since his arms were absolutely frozen in place the man simply carried him the rest of the way into the house by his elbow.

Once inside they decided to lay him on the couch. As they approached the couch, Jason was positioned at Tom's feet, between Tom and the couch. As they began to lay him down, Jason became trapped against the couch and was forced to sit down, with Tom landing on his lap. The others, now laughing at the situation, had to lift Tom's feet so that Jason could free himself.

Poor Tom... there he was, lifted high into the air, head and neck on the couch as they lifted his body and legs. He was as stiff as a board—just hanging there while Jason made his escape. Finally, Jason was out and they laid Tom back down, but now there was a new problem. Somehow in all the commotion, Tom had managed to bend slightly at the waist. So as he lay there on the couch, both his head and feet were slightly elevated in the air. When we pushed his head down his feet raised higher and if we pushed his feet down his head came up higher. We tried pushing both his head and feet down at the same time but it only made him sink deeper into the couch.

I cannot tell you the tears of laughter that were being shed as we playfully jostled him back and forth. Finally, we decided to forget it and just leave him bent. Someone commented, "He looks so uncomfortable." So someone else grabbed a pillow and pushed it under his head and neck and we left his feet be. We just didn't worry about his comfort.

Three and a half hours passed... it was very late now. Since Tom was showing no sign of coming out of whatever he was in, everyone decided to go to bed. I encouraged Mary to go home and get some rest since she had to work early the next morning, actually, in just a few hours, since it was already the wee hours of the morning. She reluctantly agreed saying, "Promise you will call me when anything changes." I promised and she left.

Jason was the last one to leave the room, so before he could get away, I pulled him aside. Not knowing if Tom was able to hear everything that was going on, and having to assume that he possibly could, I whispered, "Jason, I'm starting to freak out here…" I didn't want Tom to know how worried I was. Jason was very kind and reassuring, saying, "Everything is going to be fine." But there was a hint of uneasiness to his voice. He took one last glance at Tom, and nodded his head as if trying to reassure himself before he left for his bedroom. He walked down the long hallway, his slippers softly padding as he disappeared into the darkness.

Now it was just Tom and me. The house was calm and quiet but there was no way that I was going to be able to sleep. I made a make-shift bed from chair cushions on the floor next to him, but I never even laid down. I just sat on the cushions talking to him, gently stroking his head and saying, "Tom Caaaaalkins, where aaaare you?" There was no response. Not even the flutter of an eyelid.

Four hours had now passed. Jason reappeared with his laptop computer in hand. Apparently he hadn't gone to sleep after all. He had been searching the internet for some explanation for what was going on.

"You don't need to worry, look here," he said as he showed me what he had pulled up on his computer. There were several accounts of people who had had similar experiences. It was called a "trance." It was actually very comforting to know. It gave me something to cling to, some shred of explanation, some reason for hope. I was grateful that he had made the effort. After our talk, Jason went to bed.

I continued talking to Tom. They say that people in a coma can hear what is going on around them. So, in case he could hear, I wanted him to hear my voice and to know that I was right there beside him.

Five hours passed… Tom began to move. His feet were twitching. Then his legs began to move abruptly from side to side in a jerking motion, his upper body responding in the exact opposite thrashing motion. I flew down the hallway and knocked on Jason's bedroom door. "Jason! Jason! He's moving!"

154

We both ran back to the living room and just observed as Tom seemed to be wrestling with an unseen opponent. "What an encounter!" Jason whispered. Soon the movement stopped and he was back to being perfectly still, his arms still lifted. Nothing more was happening. I had hoped that the movement was signaling that he was waking up, but apparently not. Jason went back to bed. I knelt back down beside Tom and continued talking to him.

Five and a half hours passed... I suddenly had a thought. I hadn't prayed over him in tongues. It hadn't even occurred to me. So I began to very softly pray in tongues over him. The reason I prayed softly was not because I didn't want to awaken the others in the house. They were far enough away that it would have been nearly impossible for them to hear me. No. It was because I was videotaping it and I didn't want anyone, ever, to be able to hear me praying "in tongues."

So what's the big deal with that, you may wonder?

Because, ever since I became a Spirit-filled Christian, I had been very unsure of my own prayer language. I had heard so many people describe their experience of being filled with the Spirit as an overwhelming event, with a new language flowing out of their mouths like a mighty, rushing, gushing river, without effort or thought.

My experience, on the other hand, had been a very quiet, gentle one. When my prayer language slipped over my lips, it was with great effort and thought. Was I making it all up? Or was it for real? I never really knew for sure. And this uncertainty had been going on for more than 30 years. So, the only One I ever really let hear me pray in tongues was Jesus.

This night was no different. Since I was videotaping, I was going to be ever so whisper-quiet. But, the instant, and I mean the instant, I began to pray in tongues, Tom responded.

I could barely contain my excitement. I prayed even faster. He responded more. His head began to move back and forth. His lips started to move, as if trying to speak while coming out of a deep coma. Then, for the first time since this whole experience started, he made a sound. It was unintelligible, but at least he was making an effort to talk. You had better believe I kept right on speaking in tongues. It was the only thing that he had responded to... at all.

Now, his words were coming more easily, but they were still unintelligible. Then I realized what he was doing, he was responding to my tongues, in his own tongues!

So we had this little conversation back and forth—in tongues! Then, his eyes began to flutter, as if he were trying to open them. After a few seconds, sure enough, they opened, and then quickly closed. I kept talking in tongues.

Then he made a second attempt to open his eyes. This time they opened and stayed open. But it was clearly not a happy moment for him. In fact, it was an all-out, panic-stricken, what-on-earth-is-going-on moment.

For some reason, unknown to him, he now found himself in a quiet, dimly lit room, lying on a couch, with no one else around except me, when he had expected to be standing in the front of the brightly-lit church, surrounded by music and dozens of other people, just as he had been when this whole experience began. His mind could not comprehend what was going on and it showed on his face! I had to drop my camera and race to reassure him. "Tom, Tom! It's OK!" I said over and over.

Finally, he calmed down and fully came to his senses. "How did I get here?" were his first English words.

I quickly related the whole story to him, then ended by saying, "All I know is that nothing anybody did to you or said to you made any difference. You didn't respond to anything whatsoever until I prayed over you in tongues." Now this is my favorite part of the whole story and the part that simply blows my mind...

He replied, "No, you didn't."

"Yes, I did!" I said.

"No, you didn't," he insisted. "I heard you praying. You said, 'God, is he OK? Lord, I love him. Is he going to be all right? Are we going to be all right? Lord, where is he?'

"That's when I answered you. I said, 'I'm right here. Can't you see me? I'm OK. Why are you worried about me?'"

I just stood there with my mouth open wide as the realization began to sink in! Everything I had prayed in tongues, he had heard in English! And when he answered back in tongues, he thought he was answering in English! My prayer language, after doubting whether it was real or not all these years, was suddenly validated!

Since that time, I have loosed my tongue. If I am praying in my prayer language, I no longer hide it, feeling that mine is inferior to others. I pray with the best of them! Because the Holy Spirit hears and understands. It doesn't make any difference what it sounds like. He knows the deep things of our hearts! Even if we don't have a clue what we are praying, He does! Just as I didn't know what I was praying over Tom, but the Spirit knew, and related it to Tom's spirit.

Now I know, that I know, that I know, it is real! Here's how I know. I did not let Tom, in any way, shape, or form "hear" me express any of my concerns, because I had mistakenly assumed that he was hearing what was going on around him. I kept any and all concerns hidden from him. I quietly expressed them to others, but not to Tom. But what he heard in the Spirit, was nothing but my concerns. Wow!

To this day and I'm sure, for the rest of my life, the thought of this experience will take my breath away. Thank you, Jesus!

Now, for Tom's amazing side of the story, read on...

Tom's Side of the Story

Now that you know the natural side of the experience, I would like to share with you the experience from the spiritual side.

It was near the end of the first day of our Revival Town conference. I had been busy most of the evening doing lots of the behind the scenes work which is necessary for a conference to run smoothly. But now the meeting was winding down and so I went forward to enter into praise and worship at the front of the church. Pat was already up front so I worked into the crowd of people and stood right beside her, just to her right. As I stood there with people all around me I had my arms extended forward and slightly upward at the elbows when I felt a heat on my forearms. It was significant enough that I opened my eyes to see what could be causing it. I thought perhaps a furnace duct was blowing on me or a hot light had just come on or something.

I could see no logical reason for the heat on my arms, which was now increasing. I turned to Pat and asked, "Can you feel that?" I don't know if she responded to my question or not because the heat source was increasing enough that I turned back to face it. Still seeing no logical reason for the heat, I simply closed my eyes and whispered, "Lord, is this you?" At that moment everything went totally dark.

It was as if someone had instantly turned off all the lights, only darker. The only time I have ever experienced this kind of darkness was when we were on a family vacation and took a tour of an underground cavern. At one point, the tour guide explained that he was going to turn off the lights, and since we were now so far underground, there would be no light at all. That is the kind of darkness I was now seeing. There was no light anywhere. I turned from side to side and... nothing. Total darkness.

This only lasted a moment or two and then I began to see, off in the distance, a very dim light. It was just a pin point at first, yet in the total darkness it caught my attention. As my eyes tried to focus on it, it began to broaden. Slowly, it spread across my entire line of vision and it began to get brighter. As it intensified, I began to see very faint particles which were gold in color. The particles became brighter and as they intensified I could tell they were moving toward me. I watched in amazement as they approached until finally they were getting very close and very bright.

By now I could see thousands, maybe millions, of individual particles, each shining and shimmering in a brilliant gold color. In an instant, they were upon me and I felt my body tense in anticipation of the impact. Finally, I could see them hitting my body and swirling and curling around me as they passed. I could feel their pressure on my skin, much as it would feel to stand in the spray of a wave on an ocean beach.

Then they diminished and I watched with amazement as a new wave of particles began to form and approach, just like the first wave had done. This time I stretched my arms out to my sides and watched and waited. And just as before, the particles approached and impacted my body, then swirled and curled around me and then trailed off behind.

This harmonic wave-motion continued over and over, with each new wave just a little stronger than the previous one. They became strong enough that when I stretched out my arms and leaned into them, I could feel them lift me into the air and I would actually float on the lift of the passing particles. As they would trail off behind me, I would put my feet down and wait for the next wave to approach. Each wave continued to increase in strength and brightness. Soon, I began to realize that there was more to the golden particles than what I was feeling on my skin.

As I played and floated, I realized there was an overwhelming feeling of love such as I had never experienced before in my life. It was the pure love of God. It was totally overwhelming and all consuming. Nothing can compare to it. All the cares and worries of the world were gone. Nothing else mattered.

The love of God was all-consuming and complete. I knew that I could stay right there in that perfect love for all of eternity and never lack or want for anything more. As I played and reveled in that euphoric state, I now became aware that there was something off to my right side, just past my arm's reach. As I looked more closely, I realized that it was a being. This being was much taller than me and I could only see the legs, waist and trunk of the body. The shoulders and head were not visible to me. As I watched I could tell that the being was playing in the particles just as I was. In fact, he was glowing, just as the particles were. When the gold colored particles became brighter and dimmer, so did he. He appeared to be with the wind, and yet, not the wind. I loved the feeling of having that being there with me.

I continued to be totally overwhelmed with the experience. I don't know how long this went on because a sense of time had no bearing on anything. But there did come a point when things began to change.

I started to notice that each new wave changed from increasing with each cycle to decreasing, both in intensity and brightness. I watched in disappointment for a while as it became clear that particles were actually getting weaker and weaker. I realized that the experience was reversing itself. And if it reversed all the way to where it had started, I would be left all alone in that total darkness. The euphoric feeling of God's love would be gone as well.

At that realization I began to panic, and I have to admit, fear like I have never felt before began to grip my spirit. In desperation, I struggled for a solution to solve my dilemma. I decided that there was only one thing I could do, and that was to grab hold of the being next to me, So, I waited for the particles to die down and then just as they approached again, I planted my feet firmly and with all the strength within me I leapt toward the being and wrapped my arms around him.

From his shimmering appearance, I was not sure that I would find a solid form to hold on to. But I did, and as my arms encircled the being, I locked my fingers and held tight with all my strength. Immediately, I felt motion. It was not like the being was struggling to get away from me, or even trying to free himself from my grasp, but still… there was definite motion.

I just continued to hold on tightly, even though the effort was shaking my body wildly from side to side. After a few moments, the motion slowed, and then stopped. I could see that the gold particles were still coming in waves and now, to my delight, they were once again increasing with each cycle. The fear was being replaced with God's love once again, and I began to relax a bit, but it took several cycles of increase before I felt secure enough to release my grasp on the being. Eventually, I did release my grip, and the wind drifted me back to just-out-of-reach of the being and, just as before, we played together in God's overwhelming love.

It was at this point that something happened. I clearly heard Pat's voice. When I turned my focus to listen to what she was saying, the entire wind, being, and experience just vanished. I didn't feel fright or disappointment or anything, it was just that now my attention turned to hear what Pat was saying. I could tell she was just off to my left side, exactly where I knew she was standing in the front of the church. But she was obviously praying—and she was praying about me, and for me. I could hear her very clearly asking God, "Where is Tom? Is he alright? Is he going to be Ok? How long is he going to be like this?"

As she prayed, I could hear the concern in her voice and feel the distress in her spirit. I quickly answered, "I'm okay. I am right here. Can't you see me? I am right here beside you." Then I realized I could not see her either. I remember thinking, Lord, why can't I see her? Instantly the thought followed, Well silly, your eyes are closed. So I opened my eyes and there was Pat right where she should be, but instantly I knew something was very wrong. Where there should have been people and music and lights and church, there was nothing at all. It was all gone! I quickly closed my eyes again knowing that surely when

I reopened them everything would be back to normal. I opened my eyes the second time, and to my shock things were still wrong. I was no longer standing in the front of the church, but was now lying flat on my back with my feet slightly elevated. As I looked at Pat everything else was dark and quiet. My eyes focused first on Pat and then on the wall behind her. I could not comprehend what I was seeing, and as I began to sit up and turn my head there was no denying that everything was wrong! Panic began to grip me. I could hear Pat's voice beside me saying, "Tom! Tom! It's OK. I'm right here with you."

It took a few seconds for me to finally hear and believe her, and my spirit settled long enough for her to begin to explain where I was and how I had gotten here. Once I had my bearings, I realized that I wanted to share what had happened to me. We both tried to talk at the same time, trying to bring each other up to speed on the experience. We bounced thoughts off each other. Often, when Pat told me about things like people posing for pictures with me or like them carrying me like a plank, I would exclaim, "You are kidding me! I have absolutely no memory of that!" But, if proof of waking up in an entirely different location wasn't enough, she had pictures and videos to back it up!

I sat on the couch, looking at the pictures and watching the video clips, in utter amazement. It was like watching someone else, except that it was me! Talk about a strange feeling—watching yourself as if it were someone else. When we reached the point where our two stories began to merge together, we noticed a huge discrepancy.

The discrepancy was concerning the part where she prayed for me in tongues… I said she hadn't, she said she had, and she even had proof of it on video. Although I had heard every word in plain English, and even responded in English, it was clearly recorded, on video, in tongues.

She says that part blew her mind! Well, the whole thing blew mine. What an experience!

Pat and I have had the opportunity to share the testimony of my experience many places to many people and most of the time I end my story with this…

Have you ever heard an unsaved person make a statement like, "Oh, I don't want to go to heaven because I just can't see myself standing on a cloud somewhere strumming a harp for eternity." I have heard that, and now I can't wait to hear it again. When I do, I will tell them this story and then end it with, Heaven will be so much more than that, but even if it were not, even if you ended up upside down with your head in a bucket of sand, it would not matter. Because, when you experience God's love the way I experienced it in the trance, nothing else matters. God's love is so great, so complete, so overwhelming, and so all-consuming, that everything else pales in comparison. Heaven is going to be such an awesome place that I can barely imagine it.

I do, however, have a couple of regrets about my experience. The first is: that I could not photographically document what I saw from the spiritual side, like Pat was able to do from the natural side. I wish that somehow God had allowed me to take a camera along to capture pictures and video clips to share with others. The second is: the expression on my face. The whole time I was frozen in place, I had this sad looking frown on my face and since we have shared the pictures and videos with so many people and places, I have wished desperately that I had been smiling instead. I don't know if the Lord will ever repeat anything like this for me again, but I do know that now, when I begin to feel the Lord's overwhelming presence, I try to smile… just in case.

Tom's experience came when the Lord touched him and he responded with the question, "Lord, is that you?" He wanted further revelation about God's nature and he received it in a trance. Peter's trance came when he needed further revelation about God's plan to use him to spread the Good news. The apostle Paul said that he fell into a trance, when Jesus warned him to leave Jerusalem, because the Jews would not receive his testimony. Paul did not want to leave, but the Lord further revealed his plans: He intended to send Paul to the Gentiles, the same way he sent Peter (see Acts 22: 17-21.)

Exercise

The common thread in all these experiences is that the one who went into a trance either needed further revelation about God's plans for them or they wanted further revelation about His nature. The information was provided while they were in a trance. As an exercise, you might ask God for further revelation about His plans for you and for a deeper revelation of His nature. Although it's not as common, He may give you what you need in a trance.

Notes

CHAPTER THIRTEEN

Confirmation of Spiritual Travel

MANY PEOPLE WHO TRAVEL IN the spirit are uncertain that what they've experienced is real. This is particularly true of travel that is done in the body, and travel that happens when we're asleep. Many of these experiences appear to be nothing more than random scenes which appear in our imagination or meaningless dreams. It's natural to wonder if we're actually going somewhere and doing something, or if it's just our mind playing tricks on us.

Because they often appear to be events that are internal to us—ones that only take place in our mind—it's natural to want confirmation that we've traveled somewhere. Receiving confirmation that we've traveled in the spirit can be difficult. There is no way to know with certainty, in every case, that we've actually traveled anywhere. Sometimes however, God does arrange things in a way that provides evidence of our travels. Confirmation may come in a number of ways. Sometimes you'll pray for a person in a traveling experience and later, you might find out they were healed that same day. Occasionally, a person that you saw while traveling may notice your presence and confirm you were actually there. That's the case with the following testimony which was submitted by a friend who gave me permission to share her story, but wishes to remain anonymous.

> I first experienced spirit travel one night while on public transit. I was reading a book (not a spiritual one) and all of a sudden I saw in my mind's eye Jesus going into my parent's house. He was walking up their stairs and I got the impression that He was inviting me to go with Him. So I joined Him and as we got up to their TV room, He was touching my mom's feet and inviting me to pray with Him.
>
> After having this experience, I initially thought maybe it was my imagination, but later, I received some very encouraging news from her doctor regarding some medical tests that had been done. That gave me hope that perhaps my prayers for her with Jesus may have been an actual experience and not something I imagined.
>
> I have done this numerous times since then and I've seen some interesting visions concerning the courtroom of heaven. In one of these experiences, I was once again praying for my mom. I walked up her stairs (in my spirit) and looked in the TV room but the room was empty. I then walked down the hallway to the door of their bedroom and saw my parents in bed asleep. I blessed her and moved on. I didn't spend a lot of time there.
>
> About two or three weeks later, my parents visited me and my husband. As we were talking about spiritual things, she said she'd had a weird encounter that she thought was from "the other side." She said she was lying in bed and heard footsteps throughout the top floor of their house and when she looked over at her doorway, she saw me standing there! She rebuked the "vision" and told it to leave because she thought it was bad, and it left!
>
> For me this was a huge revelation, because, although I felt in my spirit my travels were significant to the prayers she needed, there was always a sense of doubt over whether they were real or not. Now that I've received confirmation of traveling in the spirit, I know I was not imagining this. It was real. And maybe it's something Jesus wants us to do.

Because spiritual travel is common when we are asleep, I'd like to provide a couple of examples showing how it might be confirmed. One night I received a prayer request by private message from a man named William. Here is the first message I received from him:

William: *Got a question from Kentucky—you talked with me a couple of years ago online one night (I know you don't remember) but in my seeking for more of the Father, I had a dream where I was in another country and got hurt, and the pain woke me up. I have the injury that I got in the dream, which added to the other problems I already have. How do I receive this, in your experience of God? Point me in a direction.*

Praying Medic: *So you received an injury in a dream, and then some time later, the same part of your body was injured?*

William: *I got an injury in my dream, dislocated my thumb, and woke up at that moment in pain, and I had the same injury. I just wanted some input of how this can happen.*

It was a very real dream. Like I was really there. I was in Asia operating a pre-WW II machine that threads metal stock. There was a white sheet stretched on four poles covering the machine from the sun, and Asian people going back and forth, handing me parts to load in the machine. As I was putting parts in the machine one after another, and shutting the loading doors, one of the pieces got ejected, and the loading door flew open and hit my hand, and it was the pain that woke me up. I got out of bed and went to the bathroom and my thumb was dislocated. It hasn't been right since then. That was in December.

Praying Medic: *It sounds to me as if you traveled in the spirit and you were actually there. Would you like to be healed?*

William: *Yes. I don't have insurance. I have tendon damage from that experience. Can you do that from where you are? Sorry— dumb question.*

Praying Medic: *Not a dumb question. Praying now.*

That night I prayed for his healing. Around 7:30 the next morning he sent me this message:

> **William:** *I received the prayer and I thank you, when I woke up I was expecting healing. But nothing yet! With your experience, how do I gain understanding when I ask God for it, for what He's allowing me to partake in and experience? He's bumped up my experiences and I don't know what to do? But truthfully, I think God's giving each of us that want more, a glimpse of things that are coming and urging us to keep seeking the real Christ.*

> **Praying Medic:** *To be honest, I'm not exactly sure why healing does not manifest every time we seek it.*

> **William:** *In the last hour the pain went away and my thumb's not locked up anymore. I wish I understood it, thank you.*

> **Praying Medic:** *You are welcome. I have a question about the dream you had where you were injured.*

> **William:** *Shoot.*

> **Praying Medic:** *I'm very interested in knowing how you could have received a physical injury in a dream, if you were not actually in the place you saw in the dream. I realize it's a bit of a stretch, but I have a lot of friends who actually go places in their dreams. I'm wondering if you didn't actually visit China in the dream. Did the people say anything to you?*

> **William:** *I am too. It was as real as right here. It's like you're living it, and you forget about home. They were talking in a foreign language but I understood and talked to them, as they were giving me the parts to put in the machines. I could see the palm trees and Asian grass, and even feel the humidity. Some had cone shape hats, and the younger men were without.*

> *When I was watching the machine thread the round stock, I noticed one of them was not right and reached over to stop it but it ejected from the machine and the loading door flew open and when it*

168

hit me, I screamed in pain. When I woke up, I grabbed my hand and went in the bathroom and my thumb was cocked sideways. Since an hour ago, it has been the first time that I've not had pain in a couple of months. But when I was there, I could feel the heat, feel the machine, and talk and hear with understanding. It's not a stretch. I remember like it just happened.

Three months ago something happened, but reversed. Six people visited me, talked for about 30 minutes and left. It shook me up for three days. But the difference was, I spoke their language and I don't know what I said, but they did. I'm just trying to figure things out. I can't do it, I don't try to, but I ask God to put people in my life and my wife's life that can help—so sometimes I step out and ask.

Praying Medic: *Let me get this straight... three months ago some people came to visit you at home for about 30 minutes and spoke to you. You spoke to them and they understood, but you did not know what you said?*

William: *Yes—it shook me up. I knew in the spirit what they were saying, but I didn't understand the language. They were encouraging me, telling me how God sees me. I have my grandkids over and joke around, and still play around with our children even though they're grown up, but things concerning God, I don't mess around with. But I try to understand more.*

Praying Medic: *That's quite a testimony. I've heard similar stories, but nothing quite like yours. I have one more question: I think your testimony could be used to help people understand a little more about how God works in our lives. I'm going to be writing a book on spiritual travel. I've gathered quite a few testimonies from friends and I have some of my own. I was wondering if I might use your testimony in the book. You could, of course, remain anonymous.*

William: *That's fine. You understand that I don't understand everything, but my wife and I know God is bumping things up. With her experiences and mine, we know God's getting ready for big things.*

Praying Medic: *I know that very few of us understand all the things God is doing these days. Each of us is given a piece of the puzzle and I think if we connect them together, we'll get a little better picture of what it all means.*

William: *If you use my testimony, it's fine, just use my given name—William.*

Praying Medic: *Thank you sir. I'll do that. I'm glad your thumb is feeling better.*

William: *Thank you, for the prayer.*

William's testimony is evidence that what may appear to be a dream may in fact be spiritual travel. How else can we explain a dream of being injured while working on a machine and then waking up with a dislocated thumb?

I also have a testimony of a spiritual travel experience I had while sleeping, that was later confirmed. One day I received a message from someone asking me for prayer for her pastor, explaining that he was in acute kidney failure and his doctor expected him to need dialysis soon. I replied that I would pray for her pastor. I prayed for him and for a few other people who were on my prayer list that afternoon. That night I had the following dream:

In the dream, I was with a man who needed a new kidney. He was an average-looking man, but I could see he had a surgical opening in his side. The opening was clean, with no blood present. He beckoned me to come near him and put my hand in his side and try to find his kidney. I placed my hand in the opening in his side and moved around some of his organs trying to locate his kidney. I pulled my hand out and the dream ended.

I awoke in the morning and told my wife about the dream. We talked about it and tried to find an interpretation, but I didn't understand it. (I had completely forgotten about the pastor I prayed for the previous day who needed a new kidney.) That afternoon, the friend who asked me to pray for her pastor sent me this message:

Praying Medic, I have a Praise Report! God has restored my Pastor back to health. He is to be discharged from the hospital tomorrow. Thank you for praying and thank God for your intense healing ministry. I've been reading your blog and learning a lot.

Two days later she sent me this private message:

Remember the one kidney that was severely damaged and operating at 25% and docs were talking dialysis and transplant? His wife told me this morning that when they checked his kidney again it showed it is now functioning at 100%!

When I first woke up, I wrote this off as just another dream. The only way I would have known it was a case of spiritual travel was by keeping in touch with the people involved. And that is a key point to keep in mind if you want to receive confirmation about your own travels. As you travel in the spirit, try to keep in touch with anyone you see and ask if they happened to have seen you around the time of your travels. If they confirm that they did see you or in some way sense you had visited them, you have confirmation. (You might want to keep these confirmations in a spiritual journal for future reference.)

As you travel in the spirit more often, receiving confirmation should not be as important of an issue. Most people, after they've received a few confirmations, develop confidence that their experiences are real and seldom doubt them after that point. Traveling in the spirit becomes for them another tool they know they can use when it's needed.

PART THREE
Where We Travel in the Spirit

CHAPTER FOURTEEN

Ben Swett's Testimonies

SEVERAL YEARS AGO, AFTER BECOMING interested in spiritual travel, I began corresponding with a man who has been traveling in the spirit for decades. Ben Swett is a retired U.S. Air Force Colonel and a Christian who began traveling in the spirit in 1953 and has journaled those experiences. Ben has been a gracious teacher and he's allowed me to share some of his testimonies. What follows are a few of the stories he's written over the years and posted on his website. Some are quite encouraging, while others should serve as a warning.

An Up-Trip
Ben H. Swett • Alert Barracks, Pease AFB, NH • 26 February 1964

I had an argument with my wife, over the telephone. I forget what it was about, but most likely it had something to do with the fact I was away from home most of the time, while she was stuck in a snow-bound little apartment

175

with two small children. If that wasn't the topic of that particular argument, it was much of the reason behind it—together with the fact I had chosen to stay in the Air Force.

I went to bed feeling misunderstood and more than a little sorry for myself. After all, I had to make a living the best way I could, even if my wife didn't think this was living. She didn't have to make it harder for both of us.

However, from a sense of justice, I tried to see things from her point of view, and that helped. Her arguments were logical, natural, from her perspective.

Next I tried to see both myself and my wife from some other, more objective, third person point of view. Once I did that, we both seemed pretty childish, but basically good and really quite lovely children, for all our failings.

Then quite suddenly, I realized that I could love my wife no matter what she said or did. My love did not depend on her. It only depended on my point of view... and I could choose my point of view! That insight was a revelation to me:

Love is an action not a reaction. It is a matter of choice!

Somehow, that thought had in it a vast sense of freedom, the lifting of a burden, a release. I cannot describe it. It is a feeling of liberation:

I can love her no matter what she says or does! I can love anyone—just because I chose to! It doesn't depend on anyone but me!

In that new-found feeling of joy... and freedom... and peace, I drifted off to sleep.

And suddenly, in the basement of that bomb-shelter alert barracks, with my eyes closed, I saw a night sky filled with stars—a universe of stars—just as though the two reinforced concrete floors above me had been removed and I was looking straight up into a perfect, cloudless night. But it was not the same night sky. There were stars of various magnitudes, in clusters and constellations, but they were not the ones I use for celestial navigation. Strange stars... but beautiful.

As I lay there admiring the view, I rose straight up, into that star-filled night. I felt completely weightless, and accelerated as I rose. It was a breathtaking experience, exhilarating, and more than a little frightening.

I went up toward, and then among, and then through, layer after layer of stars. But then, as I continued to rise, I approached what seemed to be a ceiling or top limit to this universe of stars, a gray area, like a roof.

I rose up into that area where there were no stars... and came up through the floor of what seemed to be a gigantic hall or courtroom or cathedral, still lying flat on my back.

The whole atmosphere of that place was awash with golden, glowing light—like a luminescent haze or fog. There seemed to be great pillars or columns along both sides and both ends of that spacious room, but I could not see the ceiling. If there was one, it was too high up for me to see in that golden glow.

Then I suddenly realized the room was full of people. I was surrounded by people, and I felt they were there because I was there—that they were gathered because I was expected—and I was embarrassed to be just lying in the aisle, so I stood up.

There were people on both sides, looking at me. They seemed to know me, but I didn't recognize them. There was an aisle between the people, stretching away in front of me as far as I could see.

Someone came to me, gently turned me around so I faced in the other direction, and started walking with me. In the distance, at the far end of the aisle in this direction, was a raised area, and a throne. Everything around the throne looked like pillars or curtains of light, reaching upward out of my range of vision.

There was a man—a king—standing on the raised area in front of the throne. Unlike everything and everyone else in this place, he glowed white— a radiant, penetrating white. I couldn't look directly at him, although I didn't know why.

My friend—because the one walking with me seemed to be a special friend—escorted me to the foot of the raised area. There were two steps. I knelt on the first step because I felt that was what I was supposed to do. The king came toward me, but I couldn't look at him.

He touched me, first on one shoulder and then on the other, with a great, terrible, sharp, two-handed, double-edged sword. I saw it clearly, on my shoulder, and fervently hoped that he wouldn't slip and cut my head off with it.

I don't think anything at all was said. When the king stepped back, I stood up, turned around, and started walking back along the aisle between the people. They all seemed to be smiling at me. And then, as I walked, the aisle became a flight of stairs leading downward, and I walked—or almost marched— down those stairs into the stars... and awoke in my bed in the alert barracks.

I lay there remembering everything that happened, and, although I was not sure it was real, or where I had been, I definitely felt that a king had com- missioned me and sent me back down those stairs to do something.

Perhaps more important, I remembered that I can love my neighbor, regardless of anything that he or she may say or do. Of that much I am certain.

This is an account of one of Ben's experiences when he was new to traveling in the spirit. As young men are prone to do, he used his ability in a way that was not wise and learned an important lesson.

Lost Track of Time
Ben H. Swett • Torrejon Air Base, Madrid, Spain • 30 April - 1 May 1961

On the night of 18-19 April 1961, my aircrew flew a B-47 from New Hampshire to Spain. That afternoon, we rode the bus downtown to look around Madrid. The next morning we went on alert, which meant we lived in the alert barracks for a week, ready to get to our aircraft immediately if and when the klaxon sounded. (The klaxon was a very loud horn that could be heard everywhere on the base.)

We got off alert on 27 April for a week of "rest and recuperation" (R & R). Because there were plenty of empty rooms in the alert barracks and we wanted to explore Madrid, we left our stuff where it was and rode the bus to town and back each day.

On Sunday, 30 April, we stayed in the barracks to rest. That afternoon, I decided to see if I could leave my body and go visit my mother in Arkansas. I sat in an armchair, told myself to return and wake up when the klaxon was tested at 6:00 p.m., and systematically turned off all the switches by which I normally operate my body. (How I did that is not the subject of this report.)

I left my body and traveled west, toward the sun. I thought I should be moving much faster, but I flew like an airplane across Spain and Portugal and out over the Atlantic Ocean. Then I somehow accelerated, to the Fayetteville, Arkansas, airport. My mother lived a few miles south of the airport. I headed south along Highway 71, but sailed right past her house. I turned around and tried again, but flew past her house again... several times. For some reason, I couldn't land there. After a while I gave up and thought about going back to Spain, but it wouldn't be easy, because I would not have the sun to follow. I wandered around northwest Arkansas for a while and then drifted into a dream.

Then— pop!—I was back in my body. The klaxon was sounding. I felt somewhat spacey and disoriented. En route to the bathroom, some of the men looked at me sideways, and one said, "Welcome back." When I started to wash my hands and face, something swung out away from my chest, over the sink, and got in the way. It was a piece of cardboard about six inches wide, hanging on a string around my neck, with a hand-lettered sign on it that read: DO NOT BURY FOR 30 DAYS.

I went back to our room, held up the sign, and asked, "What's this?"

My aircraft commander, Dick James, said, "You shouldn't scare your friends like that. You had us worried. We couldn't wake you up. And we couldn't find a heart-beat. You were still breathing—about once a minute—and I thought it might not be a good idea to move you, so we just left you sitting there. But you really should set an alarm clock, or something, before you do that."

"I did. I told myself to wake up when they tested the klaxon."

"Oh, I guess you forgot... they test it every day except Sunday. This is Monday."

* * *

It is easy to lose track of time during out-of-body travel—and it can be dangerous. How long would I have been out, if I had not set something like an alarm clock?

What would have happened if my friends had panicked and called an ambulance? If the medics couldn't awaken me, they would take my body to the base hospital, and if the doctors couldn't awaken me, they would radio for a Med-evac flight to a larger hospital—where there would be no aircraft on alert and thus no klaxon. In fact, my body could have been flown to the hospital at Frankfurt, Germany—or San Antonio, Texas—in far less time than the 26 hours I was out of it.

How many comatose people are actually out-of-body traveling?

Until recently, a body that looked that dead probably would have been buried alive. That is what almost happened to Jarius's daughter (Mark 5:35-43). Everyone said she was dead. Jesus said, "She is not dead, but sleeping." They laughed at him. He held her hand, said, "Maiden, arise"—and she did. I think she was out-of-body traveling, and he called her back to her body.

I included the previous story to show one of the dangers of traveling in the spirit. I've read similar stories from other travelers where a person became lost or had difficulty returning. In many cases the individual got lost because they were traveling out of boredom or for some purpose that had little value. When our motives are selfish or even when they're unclear, it increases the likelihood that we'll encounter problems. The next story is about a trip Ben was asked to take by God. The purpose was to travel into one of the lower spiritual realms to make contact with and potentially rescue a lost spirit. It's interesting to note that the experience began when he suddenly sensed feelings of depression for no apparent reason. The feelings he sensed were an indicator of where he was about to go.

Deep Rescue
Ben H. Swett • West Fork, Arkansas • May, 1968

I half-awoke in the early morning, stretched, and decided to doze a little longer: this was a delicious, luxurious and all too rare opportunity. It was cool and beautiful in West Fork, Arkansas. Birds were singing. I was on vacation, visiting my mother, with nothing scheduled and nothing I had to do. It was a very nice morning.

Suddenly I began to feel depressed, sad, spiritually down. For no reason I could see, I was sinking into dark and miserable moods. I tried to shake it off, but felt as though I was being pushed down into a sea of despair.

"Why?" I asked, "What is this?"

A voice-like thought that I have heard before answered, "Shhhh... It's okay."

So I went down, like something on the end of a line—a sonobouy—into something like an ocean of darkness and spiritual distress. It got worse the farther I went.

I came down through a roof into what seemed to be a large, dark room, like an aircraft hangar, with people milling around far below me, on the floor. I was still somewhere near the roof when a message came down my lifeline and I relayed it aloud: "Is everybody happy?" It sounded like a great shout in that dark place.

There was a moment's silence; then the people on the floor continued muttering and milling around, but someone swam up toward me. I couldn't see him very well, and he barely whispered: "No... no, I'm not. I'm not happy."

Another message came down my lifeline: "Would you like to get out of here?"

"Yes. How?"

An immediate message: "Think of someone you love."

Hah!—a short, harsh, explosive sound—and I heard myself add, "Or stay."

He did not reply, but he seemed to get bigger or closer or brighter. In any event, I could see him better. Then I saw a dim, glowing light come down through the roof not far away, and above it, the trace of another lifeline, shorter than mine, but stronger. This new arrival moved close to the one I had spoken with, and they seemed to contact or touch one other. Then they both moved up and out of that place.

The next message was for me: "okay, Ben... climb."

I moved up out of there, from despair through grief and guilt and regret and sorrow, and found myself lying in bed with my own tears running down my face into my ears. After a while I asked, "What was that? Was that just another lesson for me, or was it real?"

The same voice replied: "No, Ben, that was real. We got one. Thank you."

Jim Two
Ben H. Swett • Philadelphia, PA • 1983 – 1984

One of the other Directors at Defense Industrial Supply Center, an Army Colonel, stopped me after an executive meeting: "Ben, there's a family in my church who are having problems with their son, and I thought you might be able to help them."

"How so?" I had talked with him a few times about two-way prayer, and spoken to a couple of groups at his church.

"They say their son, Jim, is acting goofy—not like himself. He's always been very bright and talented and a real pleasure to them and everyone he meets. But now he seems dull and listless and almost stupid. He just can't seem to do anything right. He broke up with his girl, lost his job and his apartment, and moved back in with them. I think there may be something to what they say, because he used to sing in the choir—he had a gorgeous voice—but now he can't even carry a tune."

"Was this change slow or sudden?"

"Apparently it came on suddenly."

"When? How long ago?"

"Last summer, according to his parents. I noticed it this fall, when the choir came back from summer vacation."

"Was he sick? High fever? Has he been seen by a doctor?"

"No, he hasn't been sick in a long time. They took him to a doctor, thinking it might be a brain tumor, but the tests didn't show anything."

"Any indication of drugs? Or booze?"

"No, none of that. What has them worried now is, he's started acting scary. He quarrels with them, which he never did before. The last straw was when they found him sharpening a butcher-knife, and he said, 'I'm gonna kill the dog.' He always loved his dog. I happened to be in the church office while they were telling the minister, and I thought of you. Will you meet with Jim and see what you think is wrong with him?"

"Well... okay... I'll talk with him, but I'm not a psychiatrist, and I can't guarantee anything."

"Sure. Jim's folks know that—they just want your opinion."

I made an appointment and went to their house. Jim met me at the door—a young man in his late twenties, fairly tall, a bit overweight, with a gentle smile and a feeling of mildness about him. He said, "My folks went out," and asked, "What room do you want to use?" He seemed diffident or shy, not dynamic.

I chose the family room. He turned off the television and moved a couple chairs so we sat facing each other. I opened the conversation by asking him if he knew why I was there.

"To find out what's wrong with me."

"Well... not exactly. I'm not sure anything is wrong with you. But I understand that something has changed, something is different than it was before. Let's talk about that."

"Okay."

First, I asked him about singing. He said, "I remember singing. But I can't do it."

As we continued talking about things he remembered, he took little or no initiative in the conversation, and his responses were... slow, and minimal... but pleasant enough. He was smiling, and not aggressive. He did not seem hostile in any way.

"What about the dog?"

"His name's Bill. I used to love him more than now. I remember a couple times I was going to kill him, but I don't know why."

"How do you feel about him right now?"

"He's okay. Just a dog. Like any dog."

"So, right now, you don't love him, but you don't want to kill him?"

"Yeah, that's right. I remember doing it... sharpening the knife. But I don't remember why." As in his previous answers, he was not sullen or defensive or apologetic, just... what? Slow. Sluggish. Is he mentally retarded? Brain-damaged? An amiable loser?

I asked, "What else is different now, from the way it was before?"

He touched his head above his right ear: "I used to sit farther back in my head."

"Where do you sit now?"

"Right up here." He touched his forehead. "Right behind the eyes."

"Did this happen suddenly, from one moment to the next or one day to the next?"

"One night. From one night to the next morning. I remember that."

"Do you remember what you were doing just before it happened?"

"I remember going on a retreat. Three days."

"What kind of retreat? A church group?"

"No, Eck... an Eckankar retreat... Do you know what that is?"

His question sounded as though he didn't know what "Eckankar" meant. But I did. At this point, everything fell into place—the whole pattern. Eckankar is a group that advocates out-of-body travel. Jim went to a retreat where they taught out-of-body travel techniques. After he got home, he tried to get out of his body, and succeeded. But it was like he left his car parked with a door open and the motor running. Anyone who happened to be in the neighborhood might hop in and drive it away.

I said, "It occurs to me that you may not be the original resident in this body. That's why you have Jim's memories but not his abilities."

His eyes got wide and he started trembling all over. "I think I'm gonna wet my pants."

"Don't soil your underwear. Just focus your attention on me. I won't hurt you. I'm just going to ask for some guidance." He stopped trembling, but his eyes got even wider and his mouth hung open. I said, "You know who I'm asking, don't you? You know who I work for."

He nodded: "Jesus."

"Yes. So... okay, let's see what he has to say."

What popped into my mind was not like anything I had heard or read about before: "Three souls involved—original occupant, this one, and a bad one. Original occupant is not interested in coming back now. Strengthen this one."

I said, "This is what I got: there are three of you involved with this body. Jim One left his body and is not interested in coming back right now. You're Jim Two and not a bad person. Jim Three is the one who fights with the folks and wants to kill the dog."

He nodded, but he looked worried.

"We're not going to cast you out, because you're not an evil spirit. We're going to ask you to stay in this body, and keep Jim Three out, until Jim One decides to return."

He still looked worried. "But I don't know... if I can do that. I don't like to fight. That other one is nasty, mean. I just like to stand back and watch."

"I understand. But if you do that, the nasty one will do something terrible, and the body will wind up in a padded cell. Would you like that?"

"No."

"I think you can keep him out. Otherwise, he would take over this body all the time and keep you out. I think you're stronger than you think you are."

"Maybe... just a minute... somebody says it's not how strong... Oh, yes.

I can keep him out, because he sits where I sit, up close behind the eyes. If I don't leave, he can't sit there."

"Good. Are you willing to do that until Jim One comes back?"

"Yes."

"All right! You can be a good tenant in this body-house. Keep the bad guy out. Be good to the folks and take care of the dog. If Jim One never comes back, you can stay as long as the body lives. If he does come back, you can return it to him without being ashamed. In either case, you will have done a good thing and earned yourself some merit—something to be quietly proud about."

Tears came up in his eyes. He smiled and nodded: "I'd like that."

"Good. So that's where we'll leave it. Oh... one more thing: Remember the one who said, 'It's not how strong'—the one who explained how to keep the bad guy out? That's a good one. Listen to him. He will guide you from okay, to good, to better. Understand?"

"Oh!... Yes... I'd like that a lot."

I stood up and he stood up, smiling, with tears in his eyes. I gave him a hug and patted him on the back. He came outside with me, shook my hand before I left, and we waved to each other as I drove away.

The next day I told the Colonel that I had met with Jim, counseled him, and outlined a course of action. Now we would have to wait to see if it made any difference. I did not tell him the rest of it, because I felt that it wouldn't do him or Jim's parents any good.

• • •

I didn't hear any more about Jim for several months. Finally I asked the Colonel how he was doing.

"Oh, that's right. I've been meaning to tell you. His folks say he's doing okay. Not like he used to be, but not so goofy, and not scary. He got a job as a janitor, and keeps his room clean, and does what he's told. They all seem to be getting along pretty well."

"What about the dog?"

"They said he feeds it every day and takes it for walks. No more of that scary stuff."

"Good."

Almost a year after I spoke with Jim, the Colonel stopped me again, after a meeting. "I thought you'd like to know—things are looking up for Jim. He's got a new job that he really likes. He made up with his girl, and he's back singing in the choir again."

"How well does he sing?"

"Great!—a gorgeous voice—just like before. I don't know what you said to him, and it took a while, but something sure seems to have worked."

"Good! I'm glad."

As I turned away, I thought, May God bless you, Jim Two... You were a good tenant.

The idea that one's physical body could be inhabited by another soul is shocking to say the least. It should serve as a warning to those who practice astral projection. I have no reason not to trust Ben's integrity in reporting these stories.

You might think that Christians aren't subject to the same problems encountered by those who astral project, but I don't believe this is the case. I think we can encounter the same problems. A few years ago a friend had a dream involving another friend who is very interested in spiritual travel. Both of these friends are believers. In the dream, the friend who is interested in spiritual travel became lost while traveling out of body and could not find their way back. There was a sense in the dream that they may never return to their body. While I trust that God is able to protect us, I also believe we can do foolish things that take us outside of His protection and which could pose a serious risk to us. Traveling as we are led by the Holy Spirit is the surest way to guard against danger.

People have a wide variety of out-of-body experiences. One reason is that some use astral projection and some travel with the Holy Spirit. Another reason is that people travel to different realms of the spiritual universe, based on certain conditions at the time they travel.

During the 1960s when LSD (a psychedelic drug) was popular, it became common knowledge that you shouldn't use it if you were in a bad mood. The mood you were in at the time determined the kind of experience you would have. If you took LSD when you were in a good mood, you'd have a pleasant experience, but if you took it in a bad mood, you'd have a bad one. A similar principle holds true for spiritual travel.

Where a person goes when they travel in the spirit is mostly determined by what is in their heart or their desires at the moment. Desires include our attitudes toward others and toward God. Those who truly love God and others will go into the heavens (see Mat 5:8) where they experience the light, love and joy of God. If our attitudes toward God and others are indifferent, we will visit the earthly realms of the astral plane. In these realms there is very little love or joy. Those who hate God and others go down into the lower realms where they experience darkness, fear, and pain. It's always a good idea to take a close examination of the attitudes and motives of our heart before we travel in the spirit.

CHAPTER FIFTEEN

Portals

I LIVE IN ARIZONA, WHICH is home to the city of Sedona; a beautiful town nestled in the red rock cliffs which is famous for its "energy portals." People travel from around the globe in search of a supernatural experience with these portals. I've visited Sedona a number of times and I've read some of the research that's been done on the source of energy found at the portals. Most of the research suggests that the portals owe their energy mostly to a unique presence and arrangement of rocks and minerals such as iron oxide and quartz which cause circular flows of magnetic energy in certain locations.

Such portals may provide entertainment for the curious and some opportunity for spiritual travel, though testimonies of the later are difficult to find. Many people experience spiritual travel without accessing one of these portals and if you don't happen to live near one, your opportunities to use them are limited. The use of such energy portals for spiritual transport is impractical for most people. And even if they were more widely available, I don't think they're the best means to accomplish our goals. The kind of portals we have access to as believers are more powerful, more reliable, and safer than these energy portals.

As it relates to spiritual travel, a portal is generally understood to be an entry and exit point between two realms. It is really nothing more than an opening—a doorway between two places. A portal could be a passageway between the earth and heaven or between any other two places. It seems that some portals are permanent while others are temporary. A good example of a portal in the Bible is found in the fourth chapter of the book of Revelation, where the apostle John was invited to ascend through a door (or portal) into heaven to witness the things God wanted him to see and hear:

> *After these things I looked, and behold, a door standing open in heaven. And the first voice which I heard was like a trumpet speaking with me, saying, "Come up here, and I will show you things which must take place after this."*
>
> *Immediately I was in the Spirit; and behold, a throne set in heaven, and One sat on the throne. And He who sat there was like a jasper and a sardius stone in appearance; and there was a rainbow around the throne, in appearance like an emerald.*
> REV 4:1-3

This is a wonderful example of what traveling in the spirit can be like for the believer. For those who are not experienced with traveling the spirit, an excellent place to start is to understand first, that God wants us to come into His dwelling place and meet with Him. The words "come up here" go out to all of His children. If we want to enter into the heavens we must, like John, become "in the spirit," which is to say that we must become more aware of the spiritual world than we are of the physical one. Once we are aware of the spiritual world, we simply set our heart on God and expect (by faith) that He'll reveal Himself to us the way He did to John.

Whether or not you see a door open in the heavens, you can travel there any time you like. It was nice that John received a personal invitation and that the Lord showed him the doorway through which he could enter, but we have an eternal invitation. Jesus said He is the door anyone can go through if they desire to visit heaven or meet with the Father.

During Ian Clayton's early experiences, when he was about to travel to a different location, a portal would open that was ringed by fire. Sometimes a white cloud would manifest as well. This is an interesting observation, since it seems as though clouds and fire may be a sign of the existence of a portal, according to various passages from the Bible. I'd like to provide a brief overview of this subject as it may prove helpful to some readers. What we'll look at are a few places where God entered into the earth realm from heaven, creating (or opening) a portal from that realm into this one.

When God made his covenant with Abraham and walked between the bodies of the dead animals, the Divine Presence came to earth. One may assume it was through a portal. The Bible says a "horror and great darkness fell upon Abraham." Then a "smoking oven and burning torch passed between the pieces." (Gen 15:12, 17) We can note that fire and smoke manifested when the portal opened and God came through it.

When Moses met with the Lord on top of Mount Sinai, the top of the mountain was shrouded in dark clouds and lightning. Since God manifested His presence in the earth, a portal between the two realms was created. This time, it was accompanied by clouds and lightning (see Ex 19:16).

When the people of God were led by Him in the wilderness, He manifested Himself to them as a pillar of cloud by day and a pillar of fire by night (see Ex 13:21).

The book of Ezekiel describes the appearance of the Lord as follows:

> *Then I looked, and behold, a whirlwind was coming out of the north, a great cloud with raging fire engulfing itself; and brightness was all around it and radiating out of its midst like the color of amber, out of the midst of the fire. Also from within it came the likeness of four living creatures.*
> EZEK 1:4-5

In this account, the appearance of the Lord was accompanied by a cloud, fire, and brilliant light.

When Jesus was on the mount of Transfiguration, a portal was opened, which allowed Elijah and Moses to appear on the mountain and speak from their home in heaven. But then a cloud appeared as the Father spoke to the disciples. (Mt 17:5)

The point of all this is that perhaps when a portal is opened—at least one that allows God to enter into the earth realm—a sign may be present. The sign may be a cloud, smoke, fire, lightning, or some other phenomenon.

Portal Warfare

A few years ago I took a trip to Sedona with a group of friends. One of them kept in contact with a couple of his friends who suggested we ask the Holy Spirit if He had any assignments for us in Sedona. We felt as though He did. The assignment involved freeing a couple of angels who seemed to be bound by the enemy in the portal system. After discussing it and praying, we felt our task was to set the angels free and allow them to continue with their assignments. If you're wondering how an angel of God could be trapped inside a portal by the enemy, consider the fact that the angel which was sent to deliver a message to Daniel was detained by the enemy for 21 days (see Dan 10:13).

It's a dangerous policy to pick fights with spiritual powers when you don't have a clear and confirmed assignment from God against them. There are thousands of spiritual bad guys out there in every state and nation of the world that you could pick a fight with simply because they're on the other team. I don't make a habit of picking fights, mostly because I've learned from people who have picked fights that it's a good way to get a beating. When you go up against spiritual powers you're not assigned to battle, or equipped to handle, you're probably not going to win.

I agreed to get involved in this operation for several reasons: The first was that, as a resident of Arizona, I represent God's government in this region. I'm not exactly sure how far my governmental authority extends beyond Arizona, but I'm confident it covers the geographic area of my state. We received confirmation from two trusted prophetic friends who live outside the region (who were not in contact with each other) about what was going on inside the portal. I had my friend along, and he'd been involved in this kind of thing before. I personally invited him to be a representative of my region, which allowed him to operate under my authority as a local representative. I also invited a few dozen prayer warriors to cover us in prayer, though I didn't tell them what we were up to. I would advise anyone to put a little thought, a lot of caution, and some serious prayer into your plans if you ever decide to try something like this.

After spending a few hours shopping in town, we headed to Bell Rock, the location of Sedona's largest energy portal. I didn't know for certain if there was an immediate danger to us on this assignment. I also didn't know if our proximity to the physical location of the portal posed a danger. We suspected there could be some retaliation from the enemy and not wanting to take an unnecessary risk, we decided to keep a safe distance from Bell Rock while we engaged in our warfare. We found a public parking area about a half mile away and surveyed Bell Rock and the much larger Courthouse Butte that dwarfed it, standing a few hundred yards to the northeast. We quickly and quietly spoke our decrees of freedom over the portal.

As soon as I began speaking, I sensed a strong presence of God's glory being released. With my eyes closed, I saw a thick cover of dark clouds in the spirit that were pierced by a shaft of light. An opening appeared in the clouds that gave way to a small hole of blue sky overhead. I saw lightning strikes coming from the clouds above and a release of gold dust into what appeared to be the portal itself. This made me wonder if God had not created a portal of His own through which He entered and dealt with the situation. It was all very interesting to watch. The prayers and commands only took a few minutes. After we did our thing from the parking lot, we decided to go in for a closer look. We parked at the visitor center and hiked the trail to the base of Bell Rock. We talked about many things during our walk. I gave our friends a botany lesson on the cacti, agave, and yucca plants that surrounded us. We took a lot of photos and marveled at God's creation.

Portals as Pipelines

A portal isn't just an access point to another realm. It is also a pipeline through which the resources, revelation, and power of God flows from the heavenly realm into the physical one. When I pray for someone to be healed, the power of God flows through me into the person who needs healing. When I prophesy to them, I receive revelation from heaven about their destiny, it flows through me and I speak it into this realm. If they receive my words, there is an effect on their soul and spirit which helps move them further along in their destiny. We are portals of the kingdom of God, through which He sends His mercy, love, power, and revelation into the world.

Years ago, my wife and I had a house where we hosted small gatherings with our friends. We played music, gave each other prophetic words, and enjoyed each other's company. (I always made barbecued ribs.) During some of the gatherings, signs and wonders like gold dust would appear on people's faces and hands and it was very easy to give prophetic words, even for those who did not normally prophesy. We would often stick coins to the wall by the power of God. The manifestations of the kingdom of God always seemed to flow freely through our home. During the time we lived there, I had several people who approached me privately and asked about the portal that was visible at the top of our living room. I had never seen it myself, but to others it seemed pretty obvious. If indeed there was a portal in our home, it would explain all the supernatural things that happened there.

When I spoke at *The Gathering* in Tacoma, my wife and I booked a room at a hotel for the week we were there. After being there for three or four days and not having any dreams I became concerned. It's unusual for me to go that long without having a dream. One afternoon as I was resting on the bed in the hotel room, I heard the Holy Spirit ask, "Why don't you speak a portal into existence?"

I had not thought about portals in a long time. They were definitely not on my mind, so I was fairly certain it was the Holy Spirit speaking, and not just my imagination. I closed my eyes and spoke into the atmosphere, "I speak a portal of revelation into existence between this hotel room and the throne room of God, in the name of Jesus. Let angels and dreams flow through this portal and let nothing from the enemy come through it."

That night I had the first dream since we had been in town. In the dream, I was shown the results of the prayers of friends ten, 15, and 20 years into the future. The Lord showed me in detail how their prayers had been answered. That was only one of the dreams I had that night. There were many others. All night long I had dreams and I felt an angelic presence in the room.

While we were in town for *The Gathering,* I was talking with a group of students who were taking a course in supernatural ministry. They had been to the meeting where Steve Harmon and I taught on traveling in the spirit. One of the students asked what my wife did when I was speaking. My wife confessed that she didn't really understand what her role was. "Some people are public speakers, and others are good at healing or deliverance," she said. "I'm not sure exactly what it is I do. I just pray in tongues."

As she was speaking, the Holy Spirit said to me "She opens portals." I had never considered this idea before, so I asked the Holy Spirit what He meant. I heard Him say, "What do you think she does when she prays in tongues?"

At church gatherings and meetings, when prophetic words are given, when the sick are healed, when angels appear, and when signs and wonders manifest, it seems likely they come into the earth realm through portals. Apparently, we are the ones who open them and we can speak them into existence, if necessary. If this is true, why would we want to travel to places like Sedona to visit fixed energy portals that we know nothing about, when we can simply open an existing portal near us, or speak one into existence, if we need it? There is much that God wants to teach us about portals. As with all the information in the book, I hope you use the things you've learned in this chapter to further explore this fascinating subject.

CHAPTER SIXTEEN

Time Travel

TIME TRAVEL HAS BEEN THE subject of some of the most memorable movies in history. There's just something about it that captivates our imagination. But can we really travel in time?

Not long ago, my wife had a dream where she and I were traveling in time to alter the outcomes of certain events. Until she had this dream, I'd not given much thought to the idea of time travel, but today it seems like a much more realistic possibility. There are some obvious moral and ethical considerations that must be weighed carefully if one wants to attempt to alter the events of time. I don't intend to teach extensively on the philosophical principles of time travel. That's something I'd rather have God reveal to you personally. My goal in this chapter is to provide some instruction about how we might access the dimension of time and then share a number of testimonies that illustrate some of the things that might be possible.

Albert Einstein observed that we don't really understand what time is and how it functions. He once wrote:

> *"The distinction between past, present, and future is only a stubbornly persistent illusion."*

You might be wondering in what way the past, present, and future are "illusions." Let's take a closer look at the concept we refer to as time.

As I mentioned earlier, the physical universe has the three spatial dimensions of length, width, and height, plus the fourth dimension of time. Time itself is a dimension or a *component* part of the physical universe. It is not a part of the spiritual one. (I will not discuss it in detail here as it may only cause more confusion, but one reliable source that I read has stated that the spiritual world does have a concept that is analogous to time, but that it functions differently.)

The spiritual universe is one of higher dimension than the physical universe. If you recall my illustration of the one, two, and three-dimensional universes, you'll remember that any universe of a lower dimension has less ability to perceive, in completeness, a universe of higher dimension. The reverse is also true: a universe of higher dimension can easily perceive in completeness, a lower one.

When we view things in the physical universe from the spiritual one, we have greater access to the information contained by its dimensions, including the dimension of time. We can see the events that happen in the dimension of time at a glance. We could view all the events of our life (or the life of someone else) as if we were looking at them on a calendar. We're able to see the events of history that happened before we were born as if we were witnessing them firsthand.

Some might object to this idea, because it almost seems as if it would make us omniscient and we know that only God is omniscient. Omniscience is having a complete knowledge of all the things contained in all the dimensions of all universes without the smallest detail being omitted from one's awareness. In contrast, what we're talking about with respect to seeing events in time is having a limited knowledge of the events in one dimension of one of the universes (the physical one) pertaining to one individual. That is a far cry from being omniscient. Some may wonder what purpose God might have for giving us access to such events. Allow me to illustrate one (but not the only) purpose.

Imagine for a moment you were praying and the Holy Spirit showed you some of the atrocities that were done to Jews in prison camps during World War II. Now imagine as you continued praying, you were shown detailed information about the emotional trauma these people suffered. As you pray, you ask what the Lord wants you to do with the information and you receive the impression that He wants you to pray for healing of emotional trauma for both the victims and their captors. Is it unreasonable to think that God might show you in eternity something He wants to have changed in the realm of time and ask you to pray that His will would be done?

We are only aware of and only affected by the dimension of time while we are operating in the physical universe. Once we leave the physical universe, the dimension of time still exists, but it no longer has power over us. Traveling in time then is merely an issue of which universe we're operating in. If we happen to be operating in the physical one, then time has its way with us. But when we're operating in the spiritual one, time loses its control. When we travel in the spirit, whether in a dream, by translation, translocation, or in a trance, we're operating outside the dimension of time.

Let me provide an illustration of what it looks like to gain access to information over a broad range of time. In the previous chapter I mentioned the dream I had where I saw the way in which God answered the prayers of people ten and even fifteen years in the future. How did I get access to this information? I simply entered the spiritual world and it became available to me. How did I enter the spiritual world? If you remember, this "dream" came the night I spoke a portal into existence. Merely creating the portal wasn't enough. I had to enter the spiritual world through it to receive the information God wanted me to have.

Because the spiritual universe is a higher dimension than the physical one, anything that happens in the spiritual has the potential to affect something in the physical. The physical is subordinate to the spiritual. If we were to create a new lung in the spiritual universe, it might manifest in the physical as a new lung in a person who needs one. If events in time were to be altered in the spiritual, we would expect a corresponding change in the physical. If one were to, in the spiritual world, identify the corrupted DNA of a person with a birth defect, and alter it so as to correct the defect, we would expect that individual to be healed of the birth defect, even though (from the physical perspective) it would require us to travel to a time before the person was born.

This may be difficult to imagine when we apply the constraints of time to the problem but it's fairly easy to envision once they are removed. The point being that although we often perceive time to be a concrete, immutable force, it is easily altered when the dimension of the spirit is factored in. Now let's examine what it looks like to have time altered in our daily lives. We'll begin with another testimony from Ben Swett. This was his first experience of traveling in the spirit, which happened in 1953 when he was in college:

Preview
Ben H. Swett • Fayetteville, Arkansas • April 1953

In years past, the seven days before new members were initiated into my college fraternity had been called "hell week," but by the time I came along, hazing had been replaced by an ordeal of cleaning, painting and repairing the fraternity house, and "hell week" had been revised to "help week." Nevertheless, it still meant long hours, hard work and very little sleep.

About two o'clock in the morning of the last day, I was supposed to be mopping the upstairs hall, but I was worn out. I had slept no more than five hours out of the last forty-eight, and the previous forty-eight had not been much better. So, when the members who were supposed to keep me working went downstairs for a cup of coffee, I leaned against a door jamb and shut my eyes.

Suddenly, I felt a very funny sensation under my feet, as though I was walking on coarse gravel. It crunched underfoot. Then I felt there were other people around me—that we were walking across a graveled area, toward a building I did not recognize. We went around the corner of the building and up a flight of stairs—iron stairs, like a fire escape, attached to the outside of the building. I knew that I had never been in this place before.

We entered a door on the second floor of the building, and then sat on a wooden bench in a long, narrow room. I waited for what seemed like quite a long time, during which, one after another, the pledges sitting at my right were escorted out of the room. Then it was my turn. I was taken out of that room into a large, square room where older members of my fraternity sat behind tables, in front of me and at each side. They began speaking to me and asking me questions. At one point, someone gave me a sword and told me something I was supposed to do with it. A little later he came to take the sword away from me; I raised the tip of the sword slightly, pointing it toward his feet, and he stepped back. I reversed the sword and handed it to him, hilt first. Then I was led out of the big room, back into the narrow room—and suddenly awoke to find myself leaning against the doorjamb in the fraternity house with a mop in my hands.

Wow! I thought—that was strange. I must be so tired I'm having hallucinations. Then I heard the members coming back upstairs, so I got busy with the mop. After a few more chores around the house, I was told to take a shower, put on some decent clothes, and be ready for breakfast at six o'clock. After breakfast, the members told us to get in their cars, so they could take us to the local Masonic Temple for the initiation ceremony. That surprised me because I had assumed the initiation would be held in the fraternity house.

We parked in a section of town I was not familiar with, got out of the cars and started walking across a parking lot in the half-light of dawn. Then I heard and felt something crunching under my feet. The parking lot was paved with gravel. Startled, I looked up and saw the outline of the same building I had seen in my dream five hours earlier. I wondered if there would be an outdoor stairway around the corner of that building, and there it was.

The entire next hour followed my dream precisely, even to the matter of the sword and what I did with it. I went through that hour in a sort of bemused detachment. The thought crossed my mind that I could break out of this sequence any time I chose, simply by doing something different than I had done in the dream, but I went along with it, just doing what I did next in the dream, to see how far this precise repetition of the dream would continue.

It lasted to the same moment at which I had popped out of the dream—just after I was escorted out of the room where the initiation took place, back into the narrow waiting room. This time I didn't wake up and find myself leaning against a doorjamb holding a mop. I sat and waited while the rest of the pledges went through their initiation, and then we all went back to the fraternity house.

I thought my little brush with prevision was interesting, but just my imagination. However, later that day two older members of my fraternity came up to me (separately) and asked me if I had gone through that initiation before.

I said, "No, why?" Both of them answered in essentially the same words: "Because all through the ceremony you kept looking at me just before it was my turn to speak. How did you know it was my turn next?"

I replied with some trivial remark, such as, "Oh, maybe my ESP was working," and let it go at that. What else could I say? Could I tell them I had gone through the whole ceremony five hours previously—in a dream—while standing up, leaning against a doorjamb, holding a mop? Not hardly.

But I have wondered about it. Is time a straight line from the past, through the present, into the future? Or is it like the grooves of a phonograph record, where we might skip a groove and experience some things in advance? But if we can skip a groove, what about free will? Could I actually have changed the whole sequence just by doing something different?

I don't know. The possibilities boggle my mind. But I do know I went through that initiation ceremony in advance, in a dream, so when I read of previsions in the Bible or elsewhere, I tend to think those reports might be true. Granted, five hours is not a long time, but it was long enough to teach me that such things are possible.

I have many friends who have experienced what I would call "alterations in time." Some have had time altered by just a few minutes, while others appear to have traveled thousands of years in time. One of the most common ways in which God seems to alter time is when He shortens the time it takes for someone to drive to a certain place. Many of the testimonies I've heard involve a three or four hour-long drive being completed in less than one hour. In these cases, it appears as if God's purpose for altering time is to provide us with additional time to accomplish the things we need to do. But sometimes there is a different purpose, as illustrated in our next story.

My wife drives me to work every day. We take the same route and it nearly always takes us the same amount of time: between 17 and 18 minutes. We usually leave our house at 5:35 am, which gets me to work around 5:52 am. One morning, we left the house at 5:43 am. It was about eight minutes later than I like to leave, but it should have put us at the station at 6:00 am—the exact time that my shift starts. We had been driving for about ten minutes, when I looked at the clock on the dash of the car. The time it showed indicated we had left the house just four minutes ago. I pulled my phone out of my pocket to check the time, thinking maybe the clock in the car was wrong, but it showed the same time: 5:47 am—only four minutes after we left the house. Even in light traffic with solid green lights it's impossible to drive the distance we covered in just four minutes without speeding. My wife grumbles if I drive fast and our local police are known for diligent speed law enforcement, so speeding is just not worth the hassle.

I couldn't understand why the time was wrong, but I didn't want to obsess over it, so I put it out of my mind. My wife and I talked about the dreams we had the night before and we arrived at the station at 5:54 am—six minutes early. I clocked in and helped my partner check off the gear.

A night crew that was coming off duty at 6:00 am came over and asked if we were going in service soon. Dispatch wanted them to take a call and if they did, it would make them work late. The EMT wanted to go home because he planned on driving his daughter to her first day of school. I told him we'd be happy to take the call.

We put the gear on the ambulance and went in service two minutes before our start time of 6:00 am. The EMT thanked me repeatedly for taking the call. We got the call information and went en route. To me, it was just another call.

Twelve hours later, at the end of our shift, the same crew came on duty again. The EMT met me at the time clock and repeatedly thanked me (again) for taking the call for him. His daughter was glad that he was able to take her to school. He made a big deal about it, but to me, it wasn't worth making a fuss over.

And yet there was this nagging question in the back of mind... how did I manage to arrive at work six minutes early?

And why?

I've been interested in learning about how God alters time. Or rather, how He alters our perception of it. I've listened to testimonies about time alteration with curiosity. To my knowledge, it has never happened to me before. If what I experienced truly was God altering time—it wasn't for my own gain, my convenience, or my amusement.

It happened because God wanted to bless someone who had an important date to keep. I found out later that the EMT's daughter suffered from separation anxiety and going to her first day of school without him had the potential to trigger an episode. If I had not arrived six minutes before shift change, he would have had no choice but to take the call and he would have gotten home too late to take his daughter to her first day of school.

I have a friend named Rebecca Clayton who writes under the name *The Supernatural Housewife*. She's seen many people healed and set free of demons over the years and has even seen food multiply miraculously. Here, she shares her experiences about our dominion over time:

> Over the last few years God has been talking to me on and off about time. How it works, and more importantly—that He can bend it at will.
>
> It all began around 2009. I was in church one Sunday and we were singing "How Great is Our God." When we sang the line "Age to age He stands, and time is in His hands" God suddenly spoke to me. "Give me your time, and I will multiply it, just as I did the little boy's lunchbox." No sooner had I written this in my journal than the speaker got up and said, "I wasn't going to preach on this today, but I really feel like we should talk about the feeding of the 5,000!"
>
> Over the next few years God and I talked about this, on and off. I was kind of stuck with the mindset that what He meant by "give me your time" was to spend more time focused on Him in worship and prayer. Of course that isn't a bad thing, but the problem is, it isn't really me. Try as I might, I'm just not the quiet, ordered, contemplative type. I'm noisy and chaotic and full of new ideas. I also have three kids, a dog, and a husband. Time is at a bit of a premium in my life! So I got stuck, thinking that I couldn't do what God wanted—give Him more of my time.
>
> Then about 18 months ago, something started happening. One morning after my family had all gone to work and school for the day, I had an appointment booked to call someone at 9:00 am sharp, on ministry business. At about 8:50 am I thought I would do a couple of chores whilst I waited for the time to come. I unloaded and reloaded the dishwasher, fed the dog, wiped all the kitchen worktops down. Then I got a bit carried away and folded a huge basket

of dry laundry and put it away upstairs. As I was finishing this, I remembered about the time and glanced at the kitchen clock. It said 8:50. I panicked because I thought that the kitchen clock had stopped and I must have missed my appointment. Running to the lounge, I checked the clock on the mantle, only to find that that, too said 8:50 am! I had completed about thirty minutes of housework, but the clock had not moved. As I marveled at this, God reminded me of those words He spoke to me years before—"Well, I did say that if you gave your time, I would multiply it."

I was floored! In that moment He stripped away layers of religiosity that I didn't even know I had built around my thinking. Giving God your time isn't about religious service or meditation. It's about acknowledging His Lordship over every area of your life and letting go of your anxieties about time. Since that day I have often seen time "bend"—though so far, I have not been able to bend it when I choose. It's as if it only happens when I'm not looking. My husband, however, made an accidental discovery recently.

One Saturday morning we decided to drive into the city for shopping. As we neared the outskirts of the city, the traffic slowed right down. It was around midday on a Saturday, so I wasn't surprised. "And it starts," I said, being a bit gloomy. No one likes sitting in traffic. But my husband corrected me.

"No, we won't get stuck. We will have a clear run." From that point on, the traffic flowed smoothly. Not only were we in the city center in no time, but there was no wait as we entered the multi-story parking garage. After we parked, we walked back past the entrance and there was a line of around fifteen cars waiting to enter! As we continued our day, we noticed the pattern repeating. The line of people waiting for the changing rooms in the department store somehow evaporated just at the point we needed it. When we came out a few minutes later there was again a long line of shoppers waiting to try on clothes. Similarly, throughout the day whenever we needed to go to the checkout, there was suddenly no one in line, where moments before there had been a long line.

At lunchtime, when we went to a diner, the waitress told us there would be a ten-minute wait for a table, but she came back to show us to our table within moments. My husband, who's not one for "fluff," was the first to remark on this phenomenon. He firmly believed that his declaration in the car cleared the way for us as we moved around the city.

These experiences have permanently altered the way in which I think about time. I used to have a stock phrase in moments of stress: "I don't have time for this." But God has been gently reminding me that in fact, I have the same amount of time as everyone else... perhaps more. It's how I view time that counts. Is it mine, or is it His?

He has also been reminding me of the power of my declaration. So if I catch myself saying, even just thinking, that I do not have enough time, I quickly correct it by thanking God that He created time, and there is always enough—because time is infinite.

I've also been pondering this: Jesus is the lamb slain before the foundation of the world (see Rev 13:8).

As believers, we are one spirit with the Lord. He lives in us, and we live in Him (see 1 Cor 6:17, Col 1:27).

So that means that just as He is outside of time, we also exist outside of time, with Him, which might explain how people report phenomena like being in two places at once.

After I read Rebecca's story, I realized I had experienced some of the same things, myself. On numerous occasions, I've entered a restaurant and been told there would be a 20 minute wait for a table, only to have the hostess show me to my seat a minute later. I've also seen long lines at checkout stands disappear as I finished my shopping and began moving toward the checkout stand. It seems God is able not only to alter time for us, but to help us make the most of it when we put it in His hands.

My friend Todd Adams had the following experience:

I was part of a small worship team and we were the only ones present at the time this happened. The man who was leading worship began singing the song from the movie *Willy Wonka and the Chocolate Factory:*

There's no earthly way of knowing
Which direction we are going
There's no knowing where we're rowing
Or which way the river's flowing

He was singing this song prophetically then the words changed and I began hearing "We don't know *when* we are going." Then I saw a clock and the hands were turning in both directions. The minute hand was going backward while the hour hand was going forward. The next thing I remember was hearing someone ask, "Won't you pray with me for one hour?" I knew I was in the garden of Gethsemane. I felt as if Jesus was talking to me, but I knew He was talking to Peter. I was standing next to a tree. Jesus was standing nearby, and Satan was standing on the other side of Him. Jesus was praying and sweating drops of blood. (I didn't see this, but I knew that was the narrative from the Bible.) I heard Satan taunting Him. He told Jesus it was a big waste of time. He said people didn't care about His sacrifice. Peter knew the importance of it, but still chose sleep, instead of spending time with Him. I could feel the despair He was trying to make Jesus feel. So I told Him Satan was a liar and that many people would benefit from the sacrifice He was about to make. I told Him He would have many spiritual children and brothers and sisters. I told Him that they would love Him and that I was there as a result of the sacrifice He was about to make.

Todd shared this testimony with his friends. A mutual friend named Kellie Gordley was so inspired by his testimony, she traveled to the garden of Gethsemane herself. This is her account of that experience:

I was at a retreat with a group of students, who were studying the supernatural. We were staying at a cabin. We had sensed angelic activity in the room most of the night. Around 4:00 am, a portal opened in the corner of the room that had a green ring of light around it. Me and a couple of friends went and stood in the portal. I said to Jesus, "I want to go to the garden of Gethsemane like Todd did." I went through the portal and found myself in the garden and after looking around for a while, I found Jesus. I told Him, "Todd Adams came here and I wanted to come here too." He seemed to understand. I told Him I was grateful that He let me come here. And I began mentioning my prophetic family: Matt, Shauna, Julie, and Melody. As I was mentioning these people, they all appeared there in the garden with me. I told Jesus, "I'm going to be here. I'm not going to let you do this alone." Then the scene became a fast-motion procession. I saw Him carrying the cross through town and I ran along beside Him. I was actually going *through* all the people who surrounded Him. I could also see all my friends there with me. I was there when He was crucified and saw Him take his last breath on the cross. While all of this was happening, the people who were still in the room said they couldn't see me anymore. They said I disappeared except for my hands, for about 20 minutes. At the end of this experience, I got to help roll the stone away from the tomb. As Jesus stepped out of the tomb, He put a ring on my finger.

Kellie heard Todd's testimony and used it as an access point for her own experience with Jesus. This is what I meant when I wrote earlier about accessing the spiritual realm through the scriptures. The same principle applies to accessing the spiritual realm through another person's testimony, a dream, or a vision. Our spirit's activities are determined by our thoughts. As we meditate and think on a particular experience, faith is built in our spirit, which allows us to engage the spiritual world and enter into our own experience.

There is much that we do not yet understand about time travel. My aim is not to provide a list of rules that must be followed but to give you a place to begin your explorations. Obviously, we can cause harm to ourselves and others if we fail to exercise Godly wisdom in these matters. I trust that if you are hearing and obeying what the Holy Spirit leads you to do, He has the ability to keep you safe. If you are not confident that you're hearing the Holy Spirit consistently and accurately, you might be wise to develop your ability to hear Him before you attempt these things.

Exercise

We now know that time travel can be done by entering into events in the spiritual world. (The caveat is to make certain that what we intend to do is consistent with the will of God.) The goal for this exercise is to spend time engaging the spiritual kingdom of God. That can be done in a number of ways. You might read Bible passages and books about saints who traveled in the spirit. In your mind, envision yourself doing the things you read about or entering into the very same events in the realm of the spirit. If someone you know needs healing, you might attempt to create the situation they need in the spiritual world and wait for it to manifest in the physical.

Many people find that they're able to engage the spiritual world when they spend time in prayer and/or worship. (Prayer can be thought of as simply communicating with God.) I have two friends who commute to work by train. Both have traveled in the spirit and in time during their commute by making a habit of focusing on God and His spiritual kingdom.

CHAPTER SEVENTEEN

Mansions

THERE ARE AN UNLIMITED NUMBER places we can visit in heaven. One of them is a building that the Bible calls our heavenly home. Jesus said we each have a home (or mansion) in heaven, which He's prepared just for us.

It is often taught that we must wait until our physical body dies before we can visit our home in heaven. This teaching comes from the belief that we are not allowed access to any of the heavenly realms until after our physical body is dead. I do not believe this view to be true and it's inconsistent with what Jesus taught. Our spirit has access to all the spiritual realms right now. It may not seem like this is the case, but our spirit was created in and it will eternally exist in the spiritual universe. Jesus told His disciples He was leaving to prepare a place for them, and that the purpose for it was so He could return and take them to be there with Him:

> *"In My Father's house are many mansions; if it were not so, I would have told you. I go to prepare a place for you. And if I go and prepare a place for you, I will come again and receive you to Myself; that where I am, there you may be also."*
> JN 14:2-3

In this chapter, we'll take a look at a few of the heavenly homes Jesus has prepared for us.

A few years ago I was taken into heaven in a dream. The dream began as I appeared in a beautiful wooded area. It was a bright, sunny day and I was moving along a path through the woods. To my right, I noticed an ocean with gently breaking waves—the kind you'd love if you were a surfer. As I traveled along the path, I suddenly made a left-hand turn and approached a simple dwelling. The front door (if there was one) was open and I immediately went inside. As soon as I entered the home, I became aware of a feeling of comfort and familiarity. There was a sense in my spirit that not only had I been here before, but that I may have actually lived here. It wasn't a recent memory, but an ancient one; my spirit swirled with glimpses and vague recollections of living here and being at perfect peace.

I instinctively began inspecting the woodwork of the countertops, cabinets, and windowsills. The shape of the molding was similar to what I had seen on earth. But the joints in the wood (if there were any) were impossible to detect. On earth, even the best carpenter, when he creates a miter joint, leaves a detectable line where the edges of wood meet. But I saw none. It's possible each item was made from a single piece of wood. The quality of craftsmanship was like nothing I'd ever seen.

The house itself was not large. A kitchen, living room, and a few other small rooms were all I could see. It was simple, yet elegant in its own way, and it suited my tastes perfectly. After inspecting the rooms, I looked up to find there was no roof. My gaze met a canopy of trees that stretched out into the heavens hundreds of feet above me. The trunks of the trees vaguely resembled those of palm trees, though they were much taller. My eyes began to inspect the leaves and branches. Even though the canopy was hundreds of feet above me, I could see each leaf in perfect detail. The leaves were composed of points of light of every color imaginable and some colors which probably don't exist in the physical world. Each one had a different shape and arrangement of colors that made it unique. I remember staring dumbfounded at the trees for what seemed like ten or 15 minutes. I could not take my eyes off of them. This is where the dream ended.

I believe God gave me a brief tour of my heavenly home. That's the only explanation I have which accounts for what I saw and felt while I was there. Some time ago, I spoke with a friend who was shown several homes in heaven while spending time with Jesus.

My friend was taken to a massive skyscraper that had black as its primary color. On the black background, there were millions of pink, flaming hearts of various sizes. He asked Jesus whose home this was. The Lord replied, "It's your wife's home," and then added "I'm making her into a monument of love."

The Lord then asked my friend if he would like to see his own home. He said he would. Jesus pointed to a building across the street that resembled an old two-story fire station. They walked over to the building and went inside. His experience was very much like mine. Everything inside the home, every minute detail, was perfect to suit his tastes. He absolutely adored it.

Jesus then asked if he wanted to see another home. He said he did and the Lord walked with him down to the end of the street. At the end of the street, there was a simple grass hut off to their left. My friend couldn't help but compare this humble home with that of his wife. He sensed the owner had somehow not achieved as much greatness or maybe had not deserved the kind of honor his wife did. Jesus looked at him. "Would you like to go inside?"

He said he would and reluctantly followed the Lord through the door. The inside was just as he expected. It was small and sparsely furnished. Then Jesus opened a trap door in the floor and asked if he would like to see the rest of the home. He followed the Lord down a stairway into a massive underground building where he saw many angels, who were busy constructing an underground mansion. The Lord looked at my friend and smiled. "Not what you expected?"

My friend and I took away from our experiences the realization that we all have a home in heaven that is perfectly suited for us. Some of us will have log cabins in the woods. Others will have chalets in the mountains. Some will have skyscrapers, and others, underground dwellings. Each person's "mansion" will be perfectly created for them to enjoy in eternity. Don't judge a book by its cover. Just as the outward shell of our physical body doesn't reveal our heart, the meager outer appearance of a heavenly home doesn't reveal its inner beauty.

Some might wonder what practical purpose there is for us to visit our heavenly home. I believe it serves a purpose similar to that of our earthly one. We might use it as a place of rest, when the busy pace of life has us exhausted and worn out. Wouldn't it be refreshing to travel in the spirit and rest in the solitude of our mansion in heaven? We might go there to meet with colleagues to strategize about something God has put on our "to do" list. We might go there to learn more about our destiny, our calling, and our gifts. I'm sure if you prayed about it, you might find a few more purposes.

We all have a home in heaven and you don't need to wait until you die to go there. It's there waiting for you. You can visit any time you want. If we don't have a chance to meet in this lifetime, you're welcome to drop by and visit me at my little home in the woods. I'll be sure to have coffee and tea ready.

CHAPTER EIGHTEEN

Heaven's Strategy Room

IF YOU THINK OF ALL the many places on earth you'll visit in your lifetime, each having a specific purpose, you'll begin to get some idea of the number of places in heaven you can visit, each also having its own purpose. There are some things we can do as believers from earth, but there are some things that can more easily be accomplished by visiting one of the many rooms in heaven. This is a testimony from my friend Del Hungerford, who is a composer of original music and a music professor at a college in the Pacific Northwest. Del's testimony is being provided to encourage you to explore the realms of heaven and find the different places God has prepared for us.

> Part of my most recent spiritual journey involves learning to see and do things in the spirit. To do this, I "practice" much like I do when going through my scales and arpeggios. Any good musician will tell you that it takes practice to be good. So, with that in mind, I decided to practice the things of the spirit.

One day while driving to work, I was listening to the *Prophetic Musical Journey,* which is a piece of music I composed. I asked God if there was a way I could receive any strategies about promoting my music. I immediately saw a vision of a large room in heaven, where angels and humans were standing around computers, looking at various charts and graphs on the walls. I had to think a bit about what this meant.

I saw a person sitting in a room all by themselves with nothing but a computer and a table. The next day while driving to work, I asked God what that scene meant. I heard Him saying something to the effect of, "That's what it's like when you do things in your own strength and don't utilize the resources I've given you."

I realized that the large room I saw was the strategy room in heaven. So I thought about it once more and again I saw the room. I walked back down the hall to the place where I first came in and saw long lines of people standing around. I got in the first line and noticed there were spiritual beings present, who were handing things out to people.

Because my focus was on what people were being given, I didn't pay attention to *who* the beings were. I saw some charts, graphs, and other related items on the walls. The people in the lines received items that I knew were specifically designed for them. When it was my turn, my items were handed to me and as I took them, they literally went into my body and became a part of me. After this happened, I got in another line. While standing in the second line, I saw the word "creativity" hovering in the air above the spirit being. Just like before, this word was literally absorbed right into my body. I got into a third line, where the being was painting people all the colors of the rainbow. When it was my turn, with each brush stroke, the colors soaked directly into my body. It was almost like the paintbrush itself became a part of me when I was being painted. I got into another line where bright lights were coming out of the being and anyone who stood in front of the light, became light themselves.

The last line that I got into had only a handful of people waiting. The being was handing out musical instruments and again, they were different for each person. I thought, how cool! And then I remembered an experience at a retreat where a musical instrument was put inside me by an angel. When it was my turn, I put out my hands to receive the instruments and again, as soon as the instruments touched my body, they became a part of me.

I saw many more lines but felt that for now, I was done. At this point, I began sharing the information with a group of friends and students who were in a class where we were learning about kingdom-based entrepreneurship. I sensed that each person would know specifically what to look for in their business pertaining to the graphs and charts. This information was intended to help their business grow. I then released an impartation of creativity for each person's gifts and talents so that what they were destined to do would come forth to its fullest. Through this experience, I realized that what is received must be released to those around us. Honestly, that was the best part of the whole experience! I knew that what I had been shown was intended for others as well. Soon after I had this experience, I began producing music in a new market that is outside of the mainstream Christian music audience.

One thing I learned from Ian Clayton and Mike Parsons is that I can go back and revisit places I've been before. So, during my practice times, when I haven't understood what I saw in a previous experience, I've gone back and asked more questions and saw more details from the initial experience. For example, I can take a closer look at my surroundings. Who's in the room with me? What are they wearing? What do their faces look like? I don't always see these things the first time, so it's good to know we can revisit the experience and get more information. What I've also noticed is that when I do go back, it's like I never left. I pick up right where I left off.

I had many questions about the first strategy room visit. It was too easy for me to believe I'd see the answers some day because that's what I'd been taught—to wait on the Lord. I'm learning that God really does want us to have answers. But it requires choosing to engage with Him to receive the answers. And once is not enough. Many times the answers come in pieces, like a puzzle that needs to be put together.

As far as "practicing" is concerned, I've realized it's no different than practicing a musical instrument. When learning a piece of music, I start somewhere and continue practicing the same thing over and over until it's well cemented in my hands (the technical passages) and then practice playing through an entire piece enough times that I can tie all sections together. For every performance, it takes several hours a day of practice. With a better idea of how to practice engaging the spiritual realm in my mind, I went up into the strategy room again and asked God to explain what I was given in each line during my first visit. I was particularly curious about the musical instruments being placed inside me. In the previous experience, I knew there was a "being" who gave me the instruments. This time, I knew that being was Father God.

I heard God say, "I was putting pipes of all kinds inside you so that your whole body would be a musical instrument; I was putting my frequency within you so that your whole body would vibrate at my frequency. That then goes into your music."

I sat there in my car with my mouth gaping open thinking, I finally get it! He heard my thoughts and smiled.

In the line where the being was painting the colors of the rainbow that were soaking into my body, God said, "Frequency is color. Color is frequency. They must work together. They were put inside you because they must be together."

Again, I thought, wow! I was seeing color and frequency meld together, much like a DNA chain and could see the importance of having both.

The papers I received? God asked me, "Remember all the work you just did getting flyers, download cards, price lists, and all that together?"

I said, "Yes!"

He responded, "I gave you those when you were in the strategy room the first time. What you needed for strategy in putting those materials together, you got when those papers soaked into you." I had this Aha! moment. I remembered how easy it was to sit and simply type up all the information for my marketing. It came so easily.

The line where people passed by the being emitting light? That was Jesus. I was reminded of Saul when Jesus appeared as a ball of levitating white light. Jesus said to me, "This light is creative light. Those who stand and accept it, their bodies become creative light. You need this creative light because of what you do. Speaking and thinking is creative and it needs to come from me and flow out of you through the river of life."

Del's visit to the strategy room illustrates the fact that we can engage the realm of heaven by meditating on a previous experience we've had.

Some may have difficulty believing that God would care about our commercial success. For many, commercial success seems almost antithetical to spirituality. To them, poverty is synonymous with spirituality and commercial success is seen as being shallow or "worldly." That view has been made popular by the preaching from many pulpits, but it doesn't accurately reflect God's kingdom.

In the parable of the talents, Jesus described the kingdom of God as like unto a man who gave his servants talents and then went on a journey. (A "talent" in this culture was a weight of silver that was used as currency.) He gave talents to each servant "according to his own ability." When the master returned, he asked his servants to give an account of what they had done with their talents. One had been given five talents. He reported that he earned his master five more. He was commended for using the talents wisely and multiplying them. Another servant was given two talents. He likewise reported that he doubled their worth and was commended just as the first servant was. The last servant was given one talent. Fearing that he might make a mistake, he did nothing with his talent and returned it to his master. The last servant was rebuked for his unwillingness to assume some kind of risk, even if it was only to put the talent in a bank and earn a little interest (see Mt 25: 14-30).

The point of this story is that each of us is given some measure of gifting, talent, and some resources over which we are given responsibility. God expects us to use our talents and gifts wisely and strategically. What He wants is for us to take some amount of risk, so that we might multiply them. What displeases Him is for us to be too cautious and avoid taking any kind of risk.

God advances His kingdom and its influence over society through people like Del. She uses her gifts to teach and record music which influences others. As she influences others, along with the music and instruction, they receive the revelation of God and His kingdom. It's not surprising that heaven's strategic plans for her involve the creation and promotion of her music. God's desire is that we would prosper in our gifting and destiny so that through the use of our gifts, His kingdom is advanced.

Michelle Myers, who shared a previous testimony about her van being translocated the distance of one mile, shared this testimony which is similar to Del's. Although she did not describe it as a visit to heaven's strategy room, she was given an experience and a piece of music that impacted her life, significantly.

> One of the most profound experiences I've ever had was the time I went to take a nap in the middle of the afternoon. All of a sudden, a bright light flashed in my room, and I felt paralyzed. I was instantly aware that I was not alone, but I couldn't turn any direction. Above my bed (I still remember it was to the upper left) the ceiling seemed to open. I saw an angel, who smiled and told me, "Do not be afraid."
>
> I then felt myself reach up in the spirit. I was transparent and able to see that my body wasn't moving. I could hear music, and then the angel spoke to me, "Come and go where the angels fly, take my hand and say goodbye. Peace will come, peace will come, come and go with me to heaven." Light enveloped me as the music grew louder. I found myself aware and awake in a place that the colors of earth could never do justice.
>
> To my left was the angel that had brought me there. To my right, I looked and saw a man, who had no wings, but I knew he was an angel. He had on a breastplate, and in his hand was some kind of musical instrument, like a trumpet. I knew he was waiting to blow it.
>
> Music was in the atmosphere, and even the frequency could be felt through my body.
>
> To make a long story short, I came back with a song, and immediately went into my home studio and recorded what happened and the song. I put it in video form. It was one of the most profound moments of my existence.

These are just a few examples of the places we can visit in heaven and the things we can do there. Heaven is a place of rest, but it is also a place where much is happening. Many of the activities of heaven are designed to train and equip us to carry out our divine assignments. As you visit heaven and its many rooms, you might be on the lookout for opportunities to upgrade your spiritual talents. You may find that as you receive upgrades to your spirit, you'll also receive an upgrade to your view of God.

CHAPTER NINETEEN

The Courts of Heaven

IN THE LAST FEW YEARS, there has been growing interest in learning how to operate in the courts of heaven. For those who are unfamiliar with the concept of traveling to or presenting cases before the courts of heaven, I'll provide a brief explanation of what the courts are and why we may want to visit them.

Heaven has a lot of similarities to earth, many of which are structural or organizational. Geological structures such as rivers, mountains, forests, and oceans existed in heaven before they existed here. The earth is a copy of all that exists in heaven, although it is an incomplete and imperfect copy.

The structures of society that we're familiar with did not arise randomly, nor were they the invention of man. The concepts of justice, law, courts, and legal proceedings existed in heaven first, and over the millennia our society learned of them and copied them. Our modern system of legal justice, although flawed in many ways, was based on the courts of heaven.

We see glimpses of the courts of heaven and their proceedings both in the Old and New Testaments. The seventh chapter of the book of Daniel gives us a brief view of God as a Judge who sits upon a fiery throne presiding over a heavenly court. In Psalm 82, the Lord says He judges among the hosts of heaven. In the book of Revelation chapter twenty, we see God judging individuals as He sits upon a white throne. Interestingly, Jesus is portrayed not just as our savior, but as our legal advocate or attorney (see 1 Jn 2:1) while Satan is portrayed as our accuser or the one who prosecutes us (see Rev 12:10).

Some who have read about so-called proceedings in the courts of heaven have objected to the idea that we may need to appear there. The most common objection I've heard is this: If we must face an accuser, who has some legal case against us, what benefit does the suffering and death of Christ provide?

It's a valid question and here is my answer:

There are essentially two main views of the suffering and death of Christ that are prominent among believers who operate in the super-natural. One view states that the death of Christ accomplished all that will ever need to be done to secure *and* enforce our victory over the enemy. This view states there is nothing we can or must do to assist in this victory. It has all been done for us—both the obtaining of and the enforcement of that victory.

The other view states that Christ's suffering and death were indeed all that was necessary to secure our *victory* over the enemy. However, this view also states that the *enforcement* of that victory has not yet been completed. Now that the victory has been won, believers must exercise their God-given authority to enforce it. This view sees believers as something like police officers.

Police officers assist in the enforcement of criminal law. They have the privilege and responsibility of apprehending and bringing to justice those who violate the laws within their jurisdiction. Their authority to enforce the law is granted by the powers of government that are above them. They do not contest issues of "right and wrong" with those who do evil. They simply exercise their authority and bring lawbreakers before the courts and allow the courts to make a ruling after weighing the evidence.

We are in many ways like the police officers of the kingdom of God. When we see demonic activity, we have the authority to intervene. We can not only stop the demonic activity, but we can bring the offending spirit or the one who was harmed before one of the courts of heaven for a ruling. If you understand this arrangement, you have some idea of how and why we can come before the courts of heaven.

In the same way that there are different courts on earth, each with its own jurisdiction, there are different courts in heaven, each designed to hear certain types of cases. Most people start out bringing cases before what is referred to as the "mobile court," which is a lower court that is suitable for hearing the most common cases we're likely to be involved in. If you are sick, being harassed by demons, or in some way oppressed by the enemy, this is where your case will likely be heard.

Now I'd like to share a couple of my own testimonies:

One day, I became sick with one of the worst viral infections I've ever had. My wife and I prayed to the best of our ability using the strategies we normally use, but the virus would not leave. We recruited our friends to pray for my healing. Despite all of this, the fever, chills, and weakness kept me in bed for four straight days.

On the fourth night of my illness, I was getting ready to go to sleep and my eyes were closed. In my mind's eye, I saw what looked like a bookcase with law books on it. This was a simple image that appeared in my mind. There was nothing mysterious about it. I say this because some people have a way of making these experiences seem extremely mystical, while my experiences have actually been rather ordinary.

As I looked at the image of the bookcase, I noticed there were a few golden light fixtures nearby. They were not immediately apparent, but the more I focused on the image, the more I began seeing subtle details appear. The scene was reminiscent of my grandfather's house. My grandfather was an attorney. Every bedroom in his house had bookcases lining the walls which held the law books he owned. Looking at the bookcase in the vision, I asked my wife, "Why am I seeing something that looks like a courtroom?"

Now, I wasn't absolutely certain that what I saw was a courtroom, much less the court of heaven. I'm often asked if there is a way to know for certain whether something we see in our mind is "real" or if it's "just our imagination." There is no way to know with absolute certainty what you are seeing in the spiritual world is "real." If there were a way, it would not require faith. We must simply choose to believe what we are seeing is real and dismiss our doubts, even if it means we might be mistaken. I could have written it off as my imagination, but I chose to believe instead that God was inviting me into the court of heaven to plead my case concerning my illness. We call this translation by faith precisely because it requires us to believe the experience is real. Based on this belief (or assumption) I made another assumption that somehow my spirit had appeared in the court of heaven.

Notice that in order to move forward on this path we must move from one assumption to another. Each new assumption is based on the previous one. Faith helps us get from one place to another or one situation to another in the spiritual world. It builds bridges that span the gaps of our understanding so our spirit may accomplish what it needs to.

Though in the vision I saw no one else, once I made the decision to believe I was in court, my next step was to believe a judge must be present and presiding over my case. It was another assumption, but it was a perfectly logical one. It would be illogical to appear in a court if there were no judge present. God is not illogical, so it was safe for me to believe a judge had to be present, even though I did not see one.

I remembered Ian Clayton saying that when you are in the court of heaven it's a good idea to call your accuser to appear with you, so I asked the court to summon my accuser. What I saw next was something like a swirling cloud of darkness that began to move toward me. After about ten seconds it appeared to be beside me in the courtroom.

Knowing that my enemy is also called the accuser of the brethren, who stands before God accusing us day and night, (Rev 12:10) I asked that the accusations against me be read. I heard nothing. But as I turned (in my mind) to look at the cloud of darkness, words like "blasphemy" and "liar" appeared to be visible in the cloud. I assumed that these were the charges against me—and the reason why the enemy felt he could afflict me with sickness. Again, I had to make a few assumptions about the meaning of what I saw. I remembered Ian Clayton saying that Jesus gave us instruction about how to deal with our adversary:

> *"Agree with your adversary quickly, while you are on the way with him, lest your adversary deliver you to the judge, the judge hand you over to the officer, and you be thrown into prison."*
> MATT 5:25

Jesus actually gave us a defense strategy in the Sermon on the Mount that can be used in the court of heaven. So I did not dispute the accusations brought against me. To do so would require me to lie and there was no way I was going to give a false testimony in the court of heaven. I remembered Ian's strategy of standing under the blood of Jesus—and using its cleansing of all his sins as a defense. So I said to the court, "I stand under the blood of Jesus, which cleanses me of all unrighteousness and makes me spotless and blameless in the sight of God."

I then remembered someone sharing a testimony about their appearance in the court of heaven. When they were asked to give their defense, they didn't know what to say. An angel suggested they should ask for the books to be opened. They made the request and an angel came forth with a book, which was then opened. So I asked for the books to be opened.

At this point, the vision I was seeing in my mind changed. I saw what looked like a stone cliff. I could see there was a small room hidden behind a secret door at the base of the cliff. I saw the door to the hidden room open and a warm glow of light coming from inside the room. Then the door shut. Next, I saw what looked like a book in front of me. It took a few seconds for the image to become clear. On the edges of the left-hand page I saw a faintly visible flower pattern. There was no decoration on the right-hand page. As I looked at the pages of the book, I could see there was nothing written on them. They were blank. It was time to make another assumption.

I assumed that the book was a record of my sins. It was an assumption that required a leap of faith, but I know what the Bible says on this issue so it wasn't a big leap. Because there was nothing written in the book, I took this as an indication that my sins had been removed from the written record in heaven. So I made a short speech to the court noting that the book showed no record of my sins, because the blood of the lamb had washed them away once and for all. I said that since my sins had been washed away, there was no basis for the affliction the enemy had brought upon me. I asked for a ruling from the court to have the sickness removed. This was where the visions of the court ended.

The fever and chills persisted through the night. In the morning the fever left only to return later in the day. By 6:00 pm my temperature was back to normal and I felt much better. I slept well that night, believing the decision from the court had taken effect. The fever never returned.

I did not see angels, a judge, or any other spiritual beings of any kind except for the cloud of darkness that I believed to be my adversary. It's not uncommon for people to see other spirit beings in these experiences, but my ability to see them was restricted. I'm not sure why I was unable to see anyone, but I suspect if there were a divine reason, it might be so that I would be forced to believe in something that was not visible. Faith is required to engage that which is not seen. Through the entire experience, I heard nothing audible. All communication was done through visions God showed me in my mind and things I either said aloud or thought in my mind. To be perfectly honest, the experience was not as thrilling or bizarre as one might expect. In many ways it was very normal. It's something I think anyone could do, given the right set of circumstances and a little faith.

While I speak as though my spirit was in heaven during this experience, my physical body never left my bedroom. Sometimes it's hard to tell if your spirit and soul are in your body or out, but with this experience, there was no doubt that if I traveled, it was only in my spirit. I felt no unusual sensations in my physical body and I spoke with my wife every few minutes to let her know what I was seeing.

My Second Appearance in the Court of Heaven

One day I received an e-mail from a friend who was starting up a new business. He and I became friends after I accepted his invitation to teach healing and deliverance to a group of his friends. His business is not an ordinary business. It has specific goals that are designed to help advance the kingdom of God. I had received a number of dreams about his business as it was starting up. It was clear to both of us that God wanted me to help him on the sidelines of his business and ministry.

My friend's fledgling business had become mired in legal problems for several months and no progress had been made toward resolving them. A major deadline was approaching in the coming week and he needed the problems resolved so the business could move forward. He asked me for prayer support and specifically, to have the obstacles removed that were keeping his business from moving forward. Having one successful case from the court of heaven under my belt, I felt like I should go there again to represent my friend and his business. I asked if he had any objections to this and he said he would appreciate me going there on his behalf.

That night as I was getting ready to go to sleep, I asked the Holy Spirit if I might come before the court of heaven to plead my friend's case. I closed my eyes and saw a small table in front of me with a book on it. Looking around (in my mind's eye) I saw a few other things that made the scene vaguely resemble a courtroom, though I did not see a judge. When I see a scene of this type in my mind and I want to draw closer to an object, I exert my will and mentally decide what direction I want to move in. In this scene, I wanted to draw near to the table where the book rested. As I will myself to move in a certain direction, the perspective of the scene changes and I move closer to whatever it is I'm looking at. The motion is something like walking closer to an object in the physical world, though it is usually without the jarring sensation you get from walking. The motions in visions I see in my mind are usually very fluid. The time it takes to complete a movement toward an object can be long or short depending on the circumstances.

I knew from my previous appearance that when you're in the court of heaven it's a good idea to call your accuser to appear with you. If you don't, he'll show up on his own. So I asked the court to summon my friend's accuser. What I saw next was something like a swirling cloud of darkness that was far away at first, but began moving toward me. After about ten seconds it seemed like the swirling cloud was beside me in the courtroom, just as in my previous experience.

I asked that the accusations against my friend be read. I heard nothing, but as I turned (in my mind) to look at the cloud of darkness, words like "deceiver," "dishonest," "greedy," and "selfish" appeared in the cloud. I assumed these were the accusations and the reasons why the enemy felt he had a reason to interfere with my friend's business. Again, I had to make a few assumptions about the meaning of what I was seeing.

During my appearance in court to have my sickness removed, I did not dispute the accusations brought against me. But I was not confronting *my* adversary this time; I was confronting a friend's adversary. So I felt like a different set of rules might be in place. Since it was my friend and not me whose case was being heard, I believed I could testify on my friend's behalf. One thing to remember when you're in court is that you have the freedom to call witnesses to testify.

I know my friend and his business dealings fairly well and I believed that the accusations against him were actually false. So I asked the court to allow me to testify on his behalf. I disputed the accusations and testified that he was a just, honest, and fair man who did not take unfair advantage of people in his business dealings.

It was time to make another assumption. I assumed that the book on the table in front of me was a record of my friend's life. Each time I've been to the court of heaven, a different book has appeared before me. Each book looked slightly different and contained writing on its pages that had to be addressed. Taking my cue from Daniel 7:10, I asked for the book to be opened. When the book was opened I was not surprised to see writing on its pages. The writing was too fine to read, but it didn't matter (to me) what it said. I already knew what I was going to do.

I know that any accusations written in the book (regardless of what they are) must be answered. Because my friend is a Christian, I knew all the negative things contained in the book had been taken away by the blood of Jesus. So I told the court, "My friend has accepted the sacrifice of Jesus to atone for his sins. He stands under the testimony of the blood that washes them all away. All the accusations against him are covered under the blood of the Lamb." After I said this, I looked again at the book and noticed all the writing had disappeared.

It was time to make another assumption. Because there was no longer anything written in the book, I took this as an indication that my friend's sins had been removed from the written record. So I made a short speech to the court noting that the book showed no record of his sins, because the blood of the lamb, slain before the foundations of the earth had washed them away. I said that since his sins had been washed away—there was no basis for the enemy to continue obstructing his business. I asked for a decision from the court to have all obstacles to the progress of his business removed, since the enemy had no cause to hold things up any longer. I asked the court to give me a scroll to that effect. Then I saw something appear in front of me that looked like a rolled up sheet of paper.

The third chapter of the book of Ezekiel opened as the prophet was shown a scroll and was instructed to eat it. He did so and the revelation on the scroll was then imparted to his spirit. In the spiritual realm, such acts can be very important, though they may seem foolish at first.

In the court of heaven, when the Judge renders a verdict and you ask for a scroll, if you see one, you can simply reach out as if you're taking hold of it and make a motion as if you are placing it inside your spirit or on your body somewhere. When I saw the scroll appear as I was representing my friend, I made a prophetic act and grabbed the scroll as if it were a physical scroll and did another prophetic act by putting it in my pocket. This was where the vision of the court ended.

I received a text from my friend later that week. He had good news. Through an unanticipated turn of events, all the obstacles that had been keeping his business from moving forward had been removed and things were now moving along nicely.

As before, I did not see any beings in this experience, except for the cloud of darkness that I believed to be my friend's adversary. I heard nothing audible. All communication was done through visions I saw in my mind and things I either said aloud or thought in my mind.

The reasons we may want to appear in one of the courts of heaven are many. We might go there to have our health (or that of a family member) restored or to remove something that is opposing the advancement of our ministry or business. The court of heaven can also be used when delivering people from evil spirits. I've heard testimonies from people who have had success in getting legal action in human courts to align with God's plans after appearing in the court of heaven. Virtually anything you're involved in that the kingdom of darkness opposes may be worth considering taking before the court of heaven.

Friends who have visited the courts of heaven have noted that the atmosphere there is generally sympathetic to our situation. Whenever one is uncertain about how to proceed with their case, they may ask for help and expect to receive it from angels, Jesus, and other beings that live there. In his book *Operating in the Courts of Heaven,* Robert Henderson provides a more in-depth treatment of this subject. He discusses the different courts in heaven and their purposes. He discusses the various entities that may testify and suggests courtroom strategies. If you plan to operate in the courts of heaven, this book may be of benefit to you.

Exercise

When you find a cause that may warrant an appearance before the court of heaven, ask the Holy Spirit if you should appear there to have the case heard. If you sense that it should be brought to one of the courts, look for anything that suggests you have traveled there, such as a bench, a judge, books, angels, evil spirits, etc. You can address the judge with your concerns, even if you do not see one present. You may hear (or in some other way sense) the presence of an accuser. It's safest not to contest what the accuser says. Simply tell the judge you stand under the blood of Jesus, which takes away your sin. Ask for a ruling that the actions of the enemy must stop. (It's impossible to give a detailed outline of how every case will proceed, but most cases can be handled in a manner similar to this.) If you run into problems, don't be afraid to ask for assistance from Jesus, the Holy Spirit, or God's angels.

CHAPTER TWENTY

The Divine Council

INFORMATION ON WHAT I REFER to as the Divine Council is difficult to find. The information in this chapter is intended to encourage you to explore this subject in your studies and if the Holy Spirit leads, to observe and participate in the proceedings of these councils. In the same way that there are multiple courts in heaven, each having its own purpose, I suspect there may be more than one Divine Council, each with its own purpose.

> **NOTE:** *As with all the information in this book, please do not take anything you read here as an inflexible doctrine or a formula which must always be observed. I'm providing a few experiences and biblical background in the hope that you might build your own understanding of the Divine Council. Michael Van Vlymen, Bruce Allen, Mike Parsons, Ian Clayton, Justin Abraham, and others are helping us develop a better understanding of the courts*

of heaven, the Divine Council, and other venues of heaven. If you're not familiar with these men, you might consider finding their teachings.

The Old Testament has numerous references to what has sometimes been referred to as the Divine Council. The council is revealed in the Hebrew word סוֹד, (sod) which refers to a council of friends, a secret counsel, or an intimate council with God. The Divine Council is typically an informal discussion concerning things that take place on earth. While a proceeding in the court of heaven usually involves a judge and witnesses who testify, the Divine Council is less formal. Jesus is usually the central figure, and He occupies a throne. Sometimes the Lord will bring up an issue with those who are present and He may authorize an action on His own, or he may allow deliberations first. Sometimes a presentation is made by a human spirit (a saint) concerning a situation they would like to see addressed. Following the presentation, there is an informal discussion where representatives from both the kingdom of darkness and the kingdom of heaven may speak. When the discussions are over, the Lord may make a ruling, or in some cases, a vote is taken among those in attendance.

1 Kings Chapter 22

Humans may visit the Divine Council either as participants or as observers. The twenty-second chapter of first Kings contains an account that was witnessed by the prophet Micaiah. I'd like to provide some background information for this story:

At the time, the nation of Israel was divided into two kingdoms, the northern kingdom, which was ruled by Ahab, and the southern kingdom, which was ruled by Jehoshaphat. Ahab was one of the most wicked kings who had ever ruled in Israel. He and his wife Jezebel taught the people to worship false gods, they killed the prophets, and did many other terrible things. Because of their great wickedness, God sought a plan to deal with them and it would come from the Divine Council.

There had been peace between Israel and Syria for three years, but now Ahab was considering attacking the city of Ramoth-gilead. He invited Jehoshaphat to discuss the battle plans and gathered his false prophets to inquire if he should go to battle. All the prophets encouraged him to go to battle, but Jehoshaphat asked if there was another prophet who could provide a word from the Lord. Ahab told him there was a prophet named Micaiah, but he always prophesied against the king's plans. Jehoshaphat asked for him to be brought in. Micaiah was summoned and was asked if Ahab should attack Ramoth-gilead. Then (in verse 15) Micaiah replied, "Go, and prosper: for the Lord is going to deliver it into the hand of the king."

The prophet said it in such a way that Ahab knew he was joking. So the king said to him, "How many times shall I make you swear that you tell me nothing but the truth in the name of the Lord?" So Micaiah replied, "I saw all Israel scattered on the mountains, as sheep that have no shepherd. And the Lord said, 'These have no master. Let each return to his house in peace.'" The prophet told the king that he (the shepherd) would be killed and the Israelites (the sheep) would be scattered (verses 16-17).

Ahab turned to Jehoshaphat and basically said, "I told you this guy never gives me an encouraging word." Ahab had just heard the truth straight from the mouth of God's prophet. But the wickedness in his heart made him susceptible to the influence of evil spirits. His preference for evil would prove to be his fatal mistake as the Divine Council was now in session and they discussed his situation. Micaiah described to Ahab what he witnessed in the Divine Council:

> "I saw the Lord sitting on His throne, and all the host of heaven standing by, on His right hand and on His left. And the Lord said, 'Who will persuade Ahab to go up, that he may fall at Ramoth Gilead?' So one spoke in this manner, and another spoke in that manner. Then a spirit came forward and stood before the Lord, and said, 'I will persuade him.' The Lord said to him, 'In what way?' So he said, 'I will go out and be a lying spirit in the mouth of all his prophets.' And the Lord said, 'You shall persuade him, and also prevail. Go out and do so.' Therefore look! The Lord has put a lying spirit in the mouth of all these prophets of yours, and the Lord has declared disaster against you."
> 1 KGS 22:19-23

Micaiah described the scene as one where the Lord was on a throne and the hosts of heaven (angels and saints) were gathered round Him. The Lord then asked a question and there was a discussion as to what should be done. Note that a representative of the kingdom of darkness was allowed to submit a proposal which could be acted upon. Micaiah stood in the council and was informed of the plan, which allowed him to accurately prophesy the event.

If you're wondering why God allowed an evil spirit to lie to Ahab through his false prophets, you must remember that Micaiah told Ahab everything that he saw in the Divine Council. He was told that his false prophets were going to mislead him. Ahab had access to the truth, but he chose to believe a lie instead. God will give us the truth, but He honors our preferences and won't force us to accept it.

One might also wonder why God would consult with humans concerning His plans for earth. God is the sovereign ruler of heaven but He has placed the administration of the affairs of earth in our hands, as the psalmist noted:

> *"The heaven, even the heavens, are the Lord's; But the earth He has given to the children of men."*
> PS 115:16

God desires to include us in the heavenly decisions that impact our planet, which is why He invites us to participate in and observe His deliberations.

Psalm 82

The 82nd psalm records a discussion among heavenly beings. This psalm has been used by Mormon theologians to suggest that they will become deities one day. But the reference to the multiplicity of "gods" found in this passage does not refer to deities like God the Father. This term refers to the hosts of heaven—both angels and the spirits of men—who are referred to in the Old Testament variously as: children of the Most High, Sons of God or merely "gods" (with a little g). None of these possess the status that is reserved for Jehovah God.

God stands in the congregation of the mighty;
He judges among the gods.
How long will you judge unjustly,
And show partiality to the wicked?
Defend the poor and fatherless;
Do justice to the afflicted and needy.
Deliver the poor and needy;
Free them from the hand of the wicked.
They do not know, nor do they understand;
They walk about in darkness;
All the foundations of the earth are unstable.
I said, "You are gods,
And all of you are children of the Most High.
But you shall die like men,
And fall like one of the princes."
Arise, O God, judge the earth;
For You shall inherit all nations.
PS 82

Zechariah Chapter 3

It is not always easy to tell where a proceeding in heaven has taken place. The third chapter of Zechariah describes a meeting that seemed to take place either in a Divine Council or in one of the courts of heaven. I say this because of those who are present and because of the way in which the events transpire. If we examine this passage we might find clues that reveal where it occurred. Here are the first two verses of that chapter:

Then he showed me Joshua the high priest standing before the
Angel of the Lord, and Satan standing at his right hand to oppose
him. And the Lord said to Satan, "The Lord rebuke you, Satan! The
Lord who has chosen Jerusalem rebuke you! Is this not a brand
plucked from the fire?"

Now Joshua was clothed with filthy garments, and was standing
before the Angel.
ZECH 3:1-2

The beginning of this passage seems more like a courtroom than the Divine Council, since Satan is present and is accusing Joshua. Verses four and five read:

> *Then He answered and spoke to those who stood before Him, saying, "Take away the filthy garments from him." And to him He said, "See, I have removed your iniquity from you, and I will clothe you with rich robes."*
>
> *And I said, "Let them put a clean turban on his head."*
> ZECH 3:4-5A

Zechariah, who is a spectator up until now, becomes a participant, suggesting that after the Lord removed Joshua's sin and his clothes were changed, that he receive a clean turban. From what I've learned about the Divine Council, this scene is more reminiscent of how those meetings are conducted. Next we'll look at verses six through eight:

> *So they put a clean turban on his head, and they put the clothes on him. And the Angel of the Lord stood by.*
>
> *Then the Angel of the Lord admonished Joshua, saying, "Thus says the Lord of hosts:*
>   *'If you will walk in My ways,*
>   *And if you will keep My command,*
>   *Then you shall also judge My house,*
>   *And likewise have charge of My courts;*
>   *I will give you places to walk*
>   *Among these who stand here.*
>   *'Hear, O Joshua, the high priest,*
>   *You and your companions who sit before you,*
>   *For they are a wondrous sign;*
>   *For behold, I am bringing forth*
>   *My Servant the BRANCH."*
> ZECH 3:5B-8

In these verses, the angel of the Lord (which seems to be Jesus) addressed both Joshua and his companions who "sat before him." Who were these companions? We know one of them was Zechariah. We don't know who the others were, but they were likely to be other human spirits or angels (perhaps both). The Lord instructed Joshua that if he walked in the ways of God and kept His command, he would be allowed to:

1. Judge His house
2. Have charge of His courts
3. Have places to walk among the hosts of heaven

If you're looking for a key to operating in the heavenly realms, here we are told it's a matter of knowing God's heart and walking in His ways. Again, this scene seems to be more reminiscent of the Divine Council than a heavenly courtroom, as a number of human spectators are present, but it could be either one.

Daniel Chapter 4

The prophet Daniel lived with the Jews who were taken captive by the Babylonian king Nebuchadnezzar. The king was arrogant and refused to acknowledge the God of Israel. Eventually, he was stripped of both his power and his sanity. Daniel was told that the removal of Nebuchadnezzar's power was a "matter by the decree of the watchers and the demand by the word of the holy ones" (see Dan. 4:17). "Watchers" is another word for angels. "Holy ones" can refer to either angels or saints, but since angels were already mentioned, it would seem to be a reference to saints. The fate of the king seems to have come up for a vote before the Divine Council. The matter in question was the king's pride and his position toward the Jews. It could be that in the same way the lying spirit was sent from the council to entice Ahab, once a decision had been made by the council about Nebuchadnezzar's fate, "a watcher and a Holy One came down from Heaven" to put the plan into effect (see Dan. 4:13).

Job Chapter 1

Since it's apparent that evil spirits are allowed into the Divine Council, it seems possible that the discussion between the Lord and Satan over the fate of Job may have taken place there:

*Now there was a day when the sons of God came to present them-
selves before the Lord, and Satan also came among them. And the
Lord said to Satan, "From where do you come?"*

*So Satan answered the Lord and said, "From going to and fro on
the earth, and from walking back and forth on it."*

*Then the Lord said to Satan, "Have you considered My servant Job,
that there is none like him on the earth, a blameless and upright
man, one who fears God and shuns evil?"*

*So Satan answered the Lord and said, "Does Job fear God for
nothing? Have You not made a hedge around him, around his
household, and around all that he has on every side? You have
blessed the work of his hands, and his possessions have increased
in the land. But now, stretch out Your hand and touch all that he
has, and he will surely curse You to Your face!"*

*And the Lord said to Satan, "Behold, all that he has is in your
power; only do not lay a hand on his person."*

So Satan went out from the presence of the Lord.
JOB 1:6-12

This scene is typical of those which take place in the Divine Council.
First, a matter is brought up for discussion concerning a nation or an
individual. Then a discussion follows until one party proposes a plan
of action. The Lord then approves the plan and an agent is sent out to
put it into operation.

Divine Council Testimony

When I began this book, and during most of the process of writing
it, I had not considered writing on the Divine Council. I had some
understanding of the Council, but I had little in the way of testimonies
to share. As I worked on the last few chapters, I received an e-mail from
a man who lives in New Zealand, who shared his experience with the
Divine Council. He allowed me to publish his testimony, but wished

to remain anonymous. There are a few things I'd like to mention as background information for this testimony:

Prior to having this experience this man had been traveling in the spirit for some time and had received mentoring from three Old Testament prophets: Isaiah, Jeremiah, and Zachariah.

I received his email, copied his testimony, then rewrote it from a third-person perspective to help make it clearer for my readers. This makes it read differently from the other testimonies in the book. I sent my version back to him and asked if it was an accurate account. He said it was and gave me permission to publish it.

Lastly, the author asked that a few details be omitted, which are noted in parenthesis.

This is my retelling of his testimony:

One night, around midnight, this man perceived the arrival of an angel in his lounge, where he had been keeping a prayer watch between the hours of midnight and 3 am. The angel had a scroll in his hand, and at first, he thought it was a new assignment. But to his surprise the angel said, "You are summoned to the Divine Council meeting. Come with me."

In the spirit, he was brought in through a set of doors, into a large room. He saw six massive pillars on the right and six on the left. Though he had traveled to various places in heaven, he had never been to the Divine Council hall before.

The angel took him to a chair, which was vacant, and then he realized he was seated with the three prophets—Isaiah, Jeremiah, and Zachariah, who had been mentoring him for some time. He noticed the hall was filled with spiritual beings and almost all had scrolls in their hands. The angel handed him a scroll and said, "Do not open it until after the prayer time is done." The angel then left.

Isaiah saw he was a bit afraid of this new place, so he put his arm around the man's shoulder and said, "This is the Divine Council Hall, a place where the Lord will hear a submission from the saints in heaven or on the earth, and will allow the representatives of the fallen angels, who roam around the earth, as you read in the book of Job, to make their say. Our God is full of love and justice. He hears both sides to the submission."

Suddenly everyone present bowed low, and he did likewise. Jesus walked into the Divine Council hall. He had on garments of brilliant gold. He wore a gold crown and held a golden scepter in one hand. Isaiah said, "When He comes to judge, He dresses as the Supreme Judge of heaven and earth." The entire congregation sang *How Great Thou Art*. The elders (he was informed by Isaiah) then presented intercessions for the heavens and the earth. The Lord then asked everyone to be seated.

Everyone then began opening their scrolls. Isaiah told him to open his. He opened the scroll and read what was on it: O Great and Majestic King of heaven and earth, of the entire universe, I bring my petition before you for the nations of (omitted) and (omitted).

That was all that was on his scroll.

He became afraid because he did not know how to petition the council on behalf of two nations he knew little about. Isaiah saw his fear and he showed him his scroll. It was identical. So were the scrolls of Jeremiah and Zachariah. They smiled at him. One of them said, "You are not alone. We are with you and we will teach you how to make your submission. You will have the next three days to make it, so seek the Lord's heart and mind for these nations. Your obedience has brought you to this place and you, like all of us, had to go through this early learning process."

Jeremiah said, "You would have read how I made my pleas to the Lord saying I was too young to present the case of the nations at the Divine Council—but the Lord put His words into my mouth. They are His words. Seek His heart and mind over the next three days and then you will be here again to make your submission. All the people in this Divine Council hall, the saints and angels, are with you and for you, and delighted to hear you. They support you and the bride of our Lord on the earth. Do not be afraid, we will teach you your submissions."

The proceedings began with a submission from one of the saints for the USA. He was not allowed to hear it. His auditory functions were suddenly shut off.

He could see that the representatives of the fallen angels were allowed to comment on the presentation. It was like they were allowed to share their side of the representation made by that saint. He then became afraid of what would happen when he made his submission, if a representative of the fallen angels made a counter argument.

The angel that brought him to the hall then came and placed his hand on his shoulder and said it was time to return. He then returned to his lounge. The time on earth that he was gone was three hours. Isaiah suggested he read a specific chapter from his book saying it would help him write his submission. Later, the prophet helped him dictate the submission.

Three nights later, Isaiah, Jeremiah, and Zachariah visited him at midnight. He was briefed by Isaiah regarding the proceedings. The angel arrived about ten minutes later and asked if they were all ready to go. He had the scroll with the submission in his hand.

In a moment they were at the Divine Council halls. This time he entered through a pair of side doors into an anteroom. He was given a cloak to wear as anyone who brought up a submission had to wear a cloak. He sat with Isaiah, Jeremiah, and Zachariah. As the Lord entered, they sang a song *You are Seated on Your Glorious Throne*. After the Lord sat on His throne of judgment, a Cherub said in a loud voice, "Bring forth the submissions to the King and Lord of the universe."

An angel approached and said, "Come with me." The angel took his scroll and led him to a place called the Well of Submission. After two other submissions were made, he was ushered in by the angel to the Submission Square—a place before the throne of God. The angel gave him back the scroll then bowed and left.

Immediately, the Holy Spirit was at his side and said, "Read out your submission to our Great and Awesome God who is King and Lord of the universe." All fear suddenly left him, and he read the submission. The Holy Spirit smiled and said, "Well done!"

The cherub then announced that if there were any counters to the submission, they should be brought forward now, otherwise our Great and Awesome God who is King and Lord of the universe, will pass His judgment.

Immediately the representative of the fallen angels spoke. (He noted it's difficult to see them as they were kept in a place of darkness, so he could not make out their countenance clearly.) "From which nation is this person that he should be allowed to speak for these nations?"

The Holy Spirit said, "It matters not from which nation he comes from, for all the nations of the earth belong to our Great and Awesome God who is King and Lord of the universe. He is an intercessor and prophet and therefore can bring a submission for any nation."

The evil representative said, "Oh I see. Then what hidden benefit does he seek that he should bring in a submission of two enemy nations? Surely he has some personal stakes in these nations, why would he want to intercede for two warring nations?"

The Holy Spirit answered: "He seeks the highest good from these two nations, both nations have biblical histories and our Great and Awesome God, Our King, has walked and lived in these two nations. As a believer and follower of our Great and Awesome God, Our King, he has every right to bring forth a submission to his King and Lord. His only personal interest in these two nations is to do the will of his God, to obey Him and to serve his Holy desires; that all men should be saved and come to the knowledge of the truth."

The evil representative said, "O that is well said. But I think he has some personal interests in those nations, some monetary benefit, some emotional gains, some hidden, evil agendas to please himself. He is, after all just another human with all its faults and failings—that cannot do anything without personal, selfish desires, unlike the One they follow and disgrace, whom they call their Great and Awesome God who is King and Lord of the universe. How often this has happened in the past, yet this Divine Council cannot learn from it."

There was a lot of discussion going on in the council meeting. He heard things like "The evil one's accusation is not right." "The submission according to the earth affairs council is right." "Isaiah could never be wrong."

Then the Lord from His throne spoke out with a roar of a lion. "Let there be silence in this house!" The silence was deafening! You could hear a pin drop. The cherub from behind the throne said, "To adopt this submission for the Lord's judgment, there must be a vote. Please stand up to agree, or remain seated if you disagree." After a short time the Cherub said, "The submission has been accepted by all the saints in this Divine Council. The evil representative has disagreed. By vote, therefore, the Divine Council has adopted the submission for divine judgment." The angel who brought him to the Submission Square came to him and took the scroll and gave it to the Cherub behind the throne.

There was again silence in the Divine Council. The Lord then spoke. "I am moved by this submission, for in it, I see my own heart for (the two nations) that is indeed very close to our hearts in this Divine Council. I therefore will do all that I desire in regard to this submission as asked for. My Word in the Holy Scriptures will stand forever, and this submission is based on My Word, therefore I will do as asked for, as I honor My Word and it shall come to pass. My Word never returns to Me void. It always accomplishes the purpose for which it is spoken. I, therefore, adopt this submission and it will be carried out according to My Word and My desires by my holy angels."

There was silence again. The angel that brought him to the submission square then came to him and said "Come, I will take you back to your chair." The Blessed Holy Spirit looked at him and hugged him and said, "Our Lord is kind and merciful. Your submission will now be done by heaven on earth. This is what the Lord Jesus meant in His prayer—Thy will be done on earth as it is in heaven. Be blessed."

He went back to his seat near Isaiah. His scroll with his submission was now heaven's will. He was amazed at the very thought of it. The Divine Council meeting was over and soon he was surrounded in the corridors by other prophets and saints. The apostle Paul said, "Well done dear saint. The battle is getting fierce. We need the saints from the earth to make their submissions in heaven in the Divine Council so that the will of God is enforced on the earth. Teach this, dear brother."

Testimonies of appearing in the Divine Council may not be numerous, but they're becoming more common. While they may stretch our theological grid, I think we ought to take them seriously and ask the Holy Spirit if we might be allowed to have similar experiences.

One day during a trip to heaven, Mike Parsons was given a brief visit to the Divine Council. (Mike refers to it as the Galactic Council.) His

observation about why he was given the experience is contrary to what one might suspect. It wasn't because God likes him more than anyone else. It was because Mike is a forerunner. He's passionate about traveling into the heavens. He's been pursuing and studying spiritual travel for decades. He's been willing to exercise his faith and believe for experiences in the heavens. God honored his faith and one of his many experiences was a trip to the Divine Council. Mike said the reason why he was allowed to go there was to see it firsthand and tell us that it exists and that it's accessible to anyone—even you.

Closing Thoughts

I've attempted to portray spiritual travel as realistically as possible. There are certainly many benefits that it offers, but there are a few dangers that need to be avoided. Much of the risk can be minimized by being connected to people you trust who can provide instruction and guidance. Ideally, you should try to find a group that has mature and knowledgeable people who can teach you what you need to know and assist you in your own journey.

For most subjects pertaining to the Christian faith, this would simply be a matter of finding a local church that teaches on this subject. At present, churches that teach on spiritual travel are few and far between. You're likely to be treated with indifference (or in some cases hostility) if you were to bring this subject up with some church leaders. Because of that, I would advise using caution before talking with church leaders about your experiences. As teaching on traveling in the spirit gains more widespread acceptance, leaders may be more willing to discuss it, but right now, such leaders will be hard to find. There are however a few churches that teach on spiritual travel. Some allow access to their services online or post their content on video-conferencing and video-sharing websites. You might consider investigating these options to find more training, and ideally, a group you can learn from.

Many of the leaders I've mentioned in this book speak publicly at locations around the world. Some have developed networks that meet to discuss spiritual travel. If you want to connect with people in your area who are learning about spiritual travel, keep your eyes open for such meetings and conferences. They might provide an opportunity to find a local group you can join. (These meetings can usually be found by checking the websites of leaders who teach on this subject.) There are also social media groups that teach on spiritual travel and practice it regularly. These groups can easily be found by searching for them. They're usually open to anyone who wants to participate in a constructive way. I would recommend finding one of these groups and learning whatever you can from its members.

I'm fortunate to have friends who are willing to share their experiences. Friends who are knowledgeable about spiritual travel were hard to find just a few years ago, but they're more numerous today. I'm active on social media. You're welcome to join me and my friends as we discuss traveling in the spirit.

And now, I'd like to address a question that many of you will want answered. I'm often asked: "Why don't I see the supernatural happen in my life the way other people do?"

When someone asks me this question I usually ask how long and how often the person has been engaged in the kind of supernatural activities they hope to experience. The answer I often receive is that they seldom attempt them.

Some of us have been taught that we must wait for God to sovereignly create these experiences for us. I don't believe that's the best way to view the supernatural. The reason why many of us never have these experiences is because we're not choosing to engage the supernatural realm, regularly.

I'd love to be skilled enough to pilot a fighter jet at Mach two without crashing it. Why don't I? It's not because I'm waiting for God to park a fighter jet in my driveway. It's because I've never taken any training to fly a jet. And until I do, my desire to fly will remain unfulfilled.

Traveling in the spirit will always come more easily to those who regularly engage the supernatural realm and it will always elude those who don't. You don't need to spend long hours engaging heaven before you can travel in the spirit. If you're a busy person, rather than setting aside a three or four hour block of time, consider setting aside just ten or 15 minutes a day, several times a week. You may be surprised at the results you'll see.

It's common to hear leaders teach that you must receive an impartation, be anointed by God or receive a special gift before you can operate in the supernatural. The testimonies you've just read tell a different story. My friends are not especially gifted. They aren't well-known ministers who preach to large crowds. They are for the most part, average people, who work average jobs. Some are retirees, some are disabled and some are still trying to understand God's plan for their life. The difference between them and anyone who is not traveling in the spirit is their passion for Jesus and their pursuit of His supernatural kingdom. If my books teach you anything, I hope they teach you that you don't need to be a spiritual superstar to have incredible experiences with God.

I hope this book has inspired you to engage the kingdom of God daily. But more than anything else, I pray it causes you to fall more deeply in love with our awesome King of the universe, whose love for you is greater than you'll ever know.

THANK YOU FOR PURCHASING THIS BOOK

For inspiring articles and an up-to-date list of my books,
go to my website, **PrayingMedic.com**.

Other books by **Praying Medic**

Divine Healing
Made Simple

Seeing in the Spirit
Made Simple

Hearing God's Voice
Made Simple

Emotional Healing
in 3 Easy Steps

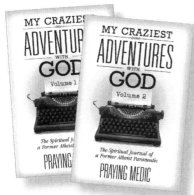

My Craziest Adventures with God
Volumes 1 and 2

A Kingdom View of
Economic Collapse

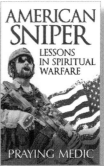

American Sniper:
Lessons in
Spiritual Warfare